Deuteronomy

A Commentary for Children

Herein is Love
COMMENTARY SERIES

Deuteronomy

A Commentary for Children

Nancy E. Ganz

Shepherd Press
Wapwallopen, Pennsylvania

Trade Paperback ISBN: 978-1-936908-455
ePub ISBN: 978-1-936908-479
Mobi ISBN: 978-1-936908-462

Shepherd Press
P.O. Box 24
Wapwallopen, PA 18660
www.shepherdpress.com
(800) 338-1445

Graphic Layout & Design:
Tobias' Outerwear for Books (www.tobiasdesign.com)
Production:

Cover Artwork: Nicora Gangi—www.machairastudio.com

Manufactured in the United States of America

To my daughter, Micaiah–a princess in Israel

CONTENTS

INTRODUCTION

Deuteronomy is the fifth and final book of the section of the Bible called the Pentateuch (from the Greek words *pente* [five] and *teukhos* [book]) or books of Moses. It is interesting that of the five books of Moses, Deuteronomy is the one most frequently quoted in the New Testament. And from the entire Old Testament's thirty-nine books, Deuteronomy ranks as the third most frequently quoted book in the New Testament (surpassed only by the Psalms and Isaiah).

The name Deuteronomy is derived from two Greek words: *deuteros* (second) and *nomos* (law). This "second law" is not another law, but the same law repeated a second time. Because of this, most children's Bible books omit Deuteronomy entirely, and it is a difficult book to make interest-catching. The book is largely repetitive—no new characters or stories are introduced, and I've already added Deuteronomy's few new details concerning earlier events to the first four books in this series. So why am I bothering to write a whole commentary on it?

Since God, in his Love and wisdom, desired to repeat the commands and events of earlier books, and since he particularly included the children in the assembly convened for all people to listen to and learn all the words of this law,[1] we can be sure that this repetition is necessary for the sake of their souls.

To help the reader's eyes not be distracted by important additional notes and scripture references all of these have been marked as endnotes which can be found at the back of the book in the section marked Notes. The notes there are sorted according to the chapter they are found in and the page numbers they are found on are marked on the header at the top of each page of the Notes section.

Explanation of Teacher's Guide

The Teacher's Guide at the end of each lesson in *Herein Is Love: Deuteronomy* can be used by any adult involved in teaching children the Bible, whether at church, home, school, or summer camp. As you prepare to teach, I urge you to prayerfully study the Scripture references given at the beginning of each lesson (some lessons do not have a Scripture reference at the beginning because they sweep the entire book), then read the lesson carefully. I've suggested visual aids, memory work, review questions, and psalms to sing, which you will want to prepare ahead of time.

Given its content, I am assuming you will use this book with older children. For my class of ten to twelve-year-olds, I gave written tests based on the review questions, kept a record of my students' grades, and handed out prizes at the end of the term for the top marks. This test-taking worked out remarkably well and made the class exciting. Because all my students wanted to score well on the test at the end of the lesson and eventually win a prize, they listened intently—which was my goal.

I've suggested several things in each lesson to rivet the children's attention and help them remember the lessons, and to connect the Bible with the real world:

VISUAL AIDS are a rich resource. Use photographs (which you can find in photography books, National Geographic magazines, old calendars, etc.), maps to point out where certain events took place, and specimens such as simple objects that play central roles in the Bible stories.

MEMORY WORK is so important as the children store up God's Word like a treasure in their hearts to help them in a time of need. I tell my students that the real reward is knowing God's Word. However as an added incentive to learn the Bible verses, I test them the following week by having them either write out their memory work or say it in front of the class.

REVIEW QUESTIONS can be used to test the children's understanding. In addition to the specific questions I've written for each lesson, there are some very important things that should be asked each time you study God's Word together:

1) What does this lesson teach us about God?

2) How does this lesson help us to live our lives?

3) How does this lesson increase our faith in God?

PRAYER applies the lesson to the children's lives.

SINGING PSALMS is a crucial but simple way for the children to store God's Word in their hearts. "Let the Word of Christ dwell in you richly as you teach . . . and as you sing psalms."[2] Singing the main psalm for each lesson several times helps the children to memorize it. You could also send home a copy for the children to sing with their families.[3]

Lesson 1

THE IMPORTANCE OF DEUTERONOMY

- Exodus 1
- Psalm 83:1–4
- I Peter 2:9, 10
- Revelation 12

Why is Deuteronomy important? For a full answer to this question, keep reading. The first lesson is entitled "Thc Importance of Deuteronomy!"

Deuteronomy is the Word of God and we know that "every word of God is flawless,"[1] and that "all Scripture is God-breathed and is useful for teaching . . . and training."[2] Deuteronomy is no exception; these words from the past can instill hope in our hearts, and hope is one of God's greatest gifts to us.[3]

God thought the book of Deuteronomy was so important that he commanded each future king of Israel to know it by heart in order to rule the country wisely. When a new king in Israel ascended to the throne, he was to "write for himself on a scroll a copy of this law. . . . It is to be with him and he is to read it all the days of his life, so that he may learn to revere the Lord his God and follow carefully all the words of this law."[4] He was to write it out entirely, read it continually, and live this word of God.

But it wasn't just the king who was to remember all the words in Deuteronomy. God commanded the whole community of Israelites to record all the words of this law as soon as they entered the Promised Land. They were to write Deuteronomy on plain field stones and set these stones up on a mountain as a monument. It was not to be a monument carved in gold or chiseled in marble or set with jewels. The value of the monument was in its precious words.

Moses told the Israelites, "Keep all these commands that I give you today. When you have crossed the Jordan River into the land that the Lord your God is giving you, set up some large stones and coat them with plaster. Write on them all the words of this law. . . . Set up these stones . . . and coat them with plaster. . . . Build there an altar . . . and offer burnt offerings on it to the Lord your God. . . . And you shall write very clearly all the words of this law on these stones you have set up."[5] The law of God in Deuteronomy was to be a permanent institution in the land of Israel, carved in stone and set on a mountain in the very heart of the nation.

As an additional reminder to the people of Deuteronomy's importance, God commanded that every seventh year the priests were to read the entire book of Deuteronomy publicly to all Israel. In this way, most people would hear the whole book read to them several times in the course of their lives. Moses commanded the priests, "At the end of every seven years, . . . during the Feast of Tabernacles, when all Israel comes to appear before the Lord your God at the place he will choose, you shall read this law before them in their hearing. Assemble the people—men, women, and children, and the foreigners living in your towns—so they can listen and learn to fear the Lord your God and follow carefully all the words of this law. Their children, who do not know this law, must hear it, and learn to fear the Lord your God as long as you live in the land you are crossing the Jordan to possess."[6] Deuteronomy was to be in the hearts of all the people as long as they lived. It was a book that would teach them and their children to fear the Lord.

The final way God commanded the Israelites to honour the book of Deuteronomy was to preserve it in a special place. "After Moses finished writing in a book the words of this law from beginning to end, he gave this command to the Levites who carried the ark of the covenant of the Lord: 'Take this book of the law and place it beside the ark of the covenant of the Lord your God. There it will remain.'"[7] Deuteronomy was so important that it was placed in the most holy place of the Lord's Tabernacle—the Holy of Holies—to remain in the very presence of God.

Moses' Final Instructions

Deuteronomy begins with the Israelites camped on the east side of the Jordan River, waiting to cross into the Promised Land to begin their conquest of Canaan. But before they made this important crossing, Moses had a few final words to say to them. Moses knew that he would soon be leaving the Israelites. He was one hundred and twenty years old and he would not live much longer. Deuteronomy contains the last words of Moses before he went to die.

These last words are especially important because Moses was a prophet—considered by the Jews to be Israel's greatest prophet, for "no other prophet arose in Israel like Moses, whom the Lord knew face to face, who did all those miraculous signs and wonders. . . . No one has ever shown the mighty power or performed the awesome deeds that Moses did in the sight of all Israel."[8] These miracles testified to the truth of Moses' words, that what he said really was from God.[9] As Moses himself declared, "The secret things belong to God, but the things revealed belong to us and to our children forever, that we may follow all the words of this law."[10]

These last words are also Moses' final battle instructions to the Israelites before they would begin the conquest of Canaan without him.[11] War was imminent and what Moses wrote in this book was designed to prepare the people of God for the battles directly ahead of them. Moses said, "Observe therefore all the commands I am giving you today, so that you may have the strength to go in and take over the land that you are crossing the Jordan to possess."[12] Again and again throughout this book Moses reminded God's people of the war that would soon take place. There is an urgency to this book, because the people were now so close to the Promised Land that they could actually see it beyond the Jordan River. They knew that very soon they must cross that river and engage in war in order to possess the land that God had given them. They must pay close attention to the words of the Lord revealed to them by Moses, because God was preparing them for war.

Christ and Deuteronomy

The book of Deuteronomy is also important because it very clearly points us to Christ. Moses declared, "The Lord your God will raise up for you a prophet like me from among your own brothers. you must listen to him."[13] About this prophet God said, "I will put my words in his mouth, and he will tell [the people] everything I command him. If anyone does not listen to my words that the prophet speaks in my name, I myself will call him to account."[14]

The Israelites waited many, many years for this great prophet—the Messiah—who had been promised to them by God through Moses. Fifteen hundred years later when Jesus walked upon the earth, they were still waiting for this prophet. When they saw the miraculous signs that Jesus did, some of the people began to say, "Surely this is the prophet who is to come into the world."[15] Jesus himself said to the Jews, "You diligently study the Scriptures because you think that by them you possess eternal life. These are the Scriptures that testify about me, yet you refuse to come to me to have life. If you believed Moses, you would believe me, for Moses wrote about me."[16] There is another amazing fact about the book of Deuteronomy that should show us how important it is. In the great battle between the devil and the Son of God, Jesus repelled all of the devil's attacks with God's Word—words from the book of Deuteronomy.[17] Jesus, King of the Jews, knew "all the words of this law"—fulfilling God's command for a king of Israel.[18] Should not these words then, which were in the heart and on the lips of the Son of God himself, be treasured in our hearts and spoken from our lips too? This is the Word of the Lord, the Sword of the Spirit, given to us in Deuteronomy, with which we can fight against the powers of darkness and wickedness, those "spiritual forces of evil in the heavenly realms."[19] When the day of evil comes, God's Word will enable us to stand firm in our faith against our great enemy, the devil.

God's Love for All of His Creation

Once an expert in the law tested Jesus with this question: "Of all the commandments in the law, which is the most important?" Jesus answered by quoting the last book of Moses. He said, "Love the Lord your God with all your heart and with all your soul and with all your mind and with all your strength. This is the first and greatest commandment."[20]

What the Jewish rabbis historically considered the least of all the commandments is also found in this book: "If you come across a bird's nest beside the road, either in a tree or on the ground, and the mother is sitting on the young or on the eggs, do not take the mother with the young. you may take the young, but be sure to let the mother go, so that it may go well with you and you may have a long life."[21] We see in this law that God was concerned even for the little birds and, as the hymn says, "If God so loves the little birds, I know he loves me too."

Is this one little law—the least of all the commandments—insignificant? No! Environmental concerns and conservation legislation are now becoming critical issues for many countries (and rightly so)—but this is ancient wisdom. The first game law protecting wildlife can be found in Deuteronomy![22] So we see that even the law considered the least of all the laws in Deuteronomy of great value to us and to our world.

But it was not just about birds that God was concerned. As in all the writings of Moses, God revealed his Love for his people in this book and assures us of it again and again. "[The Lord] made known his ways to Moses, his deeds to the people of Israel." What did the Lord reveal to Moses and to Israel? "The Lord is compassionate and gracious . . . and abounding in Love. . . . For as high as the heavens are above the earth, so great is his Love for those who fear him."[23]

Moses said to the Israelites, "The Lord your God has chosen you out of all the peoples on the face of the earth to be his people, his treasured possession."[24] Why did God set his affection upon Israel? The reason was in God, not in Israel. "It was because the Lord loved you. . . . Know therefore that the Lord your God is God. He is the faithful God, keeping his covenant of Love to a thousand generations of those who love him and keep his commandments."[25] It is in Deuteronomy that we first learn that God's covenant with his people was called a covenant of Love, because, as Moses said, "The Lord your God Loves you." [26]

Deuteronomy is a demonstration of God's great Love for his people. Like a chest filled with treasures, it is a book filled with valuable wisdom for our lives and souls. "Herein Is Love: not that we loved God, but that he loved us." [27]

LESSON 1: TEACHER'S GUIDE

The Importance of Deuteronomy

VISUAL AIDS:

My husband grew up as an orthodox Jew, and at his bar mitzvah he was given the Torah, the law, the five books of Moses. They are contained in one large volume, bound in black leather, printed in Hebrew on one page and English on the opposite page, signed by the rabbi of his synagogue, and stamped with a Star of David. Such a book would be very interesting for the children to see. Even pictures of the Torah scrolls in Jewish synagogues would interest your young Bible students.

MEMORY WORK:

"O Lord . . . your word is a lamp to my feet and a light for my path."
Psalm 119:105

REVIEW QUESTIONS:

1. Where do we find Moses' final words to the Israelites?
2. What part of the Bible is called "the books of Moses?"
3. What did God command the kings of Israel to do with this book called Deuteronomy?
4. What did God command the Israelites to do with "all the words of this law" as soon as they entered the Promised Land?
5. What did God command the Israelites to do every seven years?
6. Where was this book of the law to be kept? Why?
7. Jesus said that Moses wrote about him, although it was fifteen hundred years before the time of Christ. What did Moses say about Jesus in Deuteronomy?

8. How did Jesus answer the devil's temptations? From which book of Scripture did Jesus answer all three times?
9. What did Jesus say was the greatest commandment? Where is that commandment found?
10. What did the Jewish rabbis say was the least commandment? Where is that commandment found? Why is even this commandment important?
11. Why do you think it is necessary for us to study Deuteronomy?

PRAYER:

O Lord, our heavenly Father, we thank you for giving us this fifth book of the Bible. We thank you for revealing your Word to us through Moses and for preserving this ancient book for thousands of years for us. Please open our minds to understand the Scriptures, especially all that is written by the prophets concerning Jesus Christ. May we always love your Word and seek the truth. May we always be careful to study your Word and obey your law. Amen.

PSALMS TO SING:

These psalms all praise Scripture, urging us to trust God's word to us:

119NO . . . and 56 (2, 5, 6); 78A; 119BWX; 130AB; 138AB

Lesson 2

DO NOT FORGET

REMEMBERING EGYPT

- Exodus 2:1–10
- Acts 7:17–22
- Hebrews 11:23

In Deuteronomy, Moses used his last words to his people to retell the crucial events of their past. When he was gone, the Israelites would no longer hear his voice exhorting them to believe and obey the Lord. Moses gave the Israelites these precious words in Deuteronomy because he did not want them to forget what had happened in the past forty years. Again and again in this book Moses commanded the people of God: Remember! Do not forget! God's people were to imprint these words on their minds and impress them on their hearts; and they were to teach these words and this history to their children.

The Israelites' bondage in Egypt was a crucial time that Moses repeatedly reminded the people of, mentioning it no less than forty-six times in this book. God displayed his Love, mercy, and power in an extraordinary way when he delivered his people from Egypt, the land of their bondage, where they had experienced cruelty and slavery. Again and again Moses commanded the people to remember this significant time in their short history as a nation. Moses said, "Remember that you were slaves in Egypt and that the Lord your God brought you out of there. Be careful that you do not forget the Lord, who brought you out of Egypt, out of the land of slavery. Remember well what the Lord your God did to Pharaoh and to all Egypt."[1] "Remember that you were slaves in Egypt; . . . Remember that you were slaves in Egypt; . . . Remember that you were slaves in Egypt—and the Lord your God redeemed you from there."[2]

Why did Moses want the Israelites to remember such a painful and shameful past? They might have felt it would be better not to think about their time of misery in Egypt. Shouldn't they forget the land behind them and focus instead on the land ahead of them?

True, in Egypt they experienced misery and cruelty and slavery, but it was of utmost importance to Moses—and to God—that they remember this time lest they forget God and all he had done for them. If they remembered these words, they would know that the Lord was God, and that he had chosen them to be his very own people. They would have courage to fight their enemies and they would show compassion to those who were in bondage. It was also important that the Israelites remember who they were as a people and all that they had done against God, so they would watch themselves carefully and not continue to repeat their sinful pattern of rebellion.

Remembering the Lord

God's people must remember their deliverance from Egypt because that great event in Israel's history clearly demonstrated to them (and to the whole world) that the Lord is God—the mighty God and the only God! All the great gods of Egypt—all their splendid idols and divine rulers—were worthless, powerless, and ridiculous fakes and frauds. The false gods of Egypt proved that they could do nothing and help no one; but the Lord, the God of Egypt's slaves, had set his people free! Moses asked the people, "Has anything so great as this ever happened or has anything like it ever been heard of? Has any god ever tried to take for himself one nation out of another nation, by testings, by miraculous signs and wonders, by war, by a mighty hand and an outstretched arm, or by great and awesome deeds, like all the things the Lord your God did for you in Egypt before your very eyes? You were shown these things so that you might know that the Lord is God; besides him there is no other. . . . Acknowledge and take to heart this day that the Lord is God in heaven above and on earth below. There is no other."[3]

Knowing that the Lord was God would keep the people from believing in or worshipping any other god. Only the Lord their God, who delivered them from Egypt, was to receive their trust, love, and praise. The Lord declared in the Ten Commandments, "I am the Lord your God, who brought you out of Egypt, out of the land of slavery. You shall have no other gods before me. You shall not make for yourself an idol in the form of anything. . . . You shall not bow down to them or worship them."[4] Moses declared to the people, "The Lord your God is God of gods and Lord of lords, the great God, mighty and awesome. . . . Fear the Lord your God and serve him. Hold fast to him. . . . He is your praise; he is your God, who performed for you those great and awesome wonders you saw with your own eyes."[5]

Remembering That God Loved Them and Chose Them

God's people must remember their deliverance from Egypt because God demonstrated his Love for them by setting them free. Moses said, "Because he loved your forefathers and chose their descendants after them, he brought you out of Egypt by his presence and his great strength."[6] Again Moses taught the people of God's Love, explaining why God had set his affection upon them. It was not because there was anything in them worthy of this Divine Love. No, thankfully their salvation did not rest upon anything in themselves; God saved them because of his own grace and mercy and faithfulness. Moses declared, "The Lord your God has chosen you out of all the peoples on the face of the earth to be his people, his treasured possession. . . . It was because the Lord loved you and kept the oath he swore to your forefathers that he brought you out with a mighty hand and redeemed you from the land of slavery and the power of Pharaoh, king of Egypt. Know therefore that the Lord your God is God. He is the faithful God, keeping his covenant of Love to a thousand generations of those who love him and keep his commandments."[7]

Remembering to Obey God

God's people must remember their deliverance from Egypt so that they would obey God's laws. Moses urged the people to love God by keeping his commandments because they had seen with their own eyes how the Lord had rescued them from Egypt, and they owed obedience to the one who had freed them. God prefaced the Ten Commandments by reminding the people, "I am the Lord your God, who brought you out of Egypt, out of the land of slavery."[8] Moses told the Israelites, "Love the Lord your God and keep his requirements, his decrees, his laws, and his commands always. Remember today that your children were not the ones who saw and experienced the discipline of the Lord your God: his majesty, his mighty hand, his outstretched arm; the signs he performed and the things he did in the heart of Egypt, both to Pharaoh king of Egypt and to his whole country; what he did to the Egyptian army, to its horses and chariots, how he overwhelmed them with the waters of the Red Sea as they were pursuing you, and how the Lord brought lasting ruin on them. . . . But it was your own eyes that saw all these great things the Lord has done. Therefore, observe all the commands I am giving you today."[9]

In the future, when their children asked what the commandments meant and why God's laws must be kept, Moses told the people to recount their deliverance from Egypt. They were to say, "We were slaves of Pharaoh in Egypt, but the Lord brought us out of Egypt with a mighty hand. Before our eyes the Lord sent miraculous signs and wonders—great and terrible—upon Egypt and Pharaoh and his whole household. But the Lord brought us out from there to bring us in and give us the land he promised on oath to our forefathers. The Lord commanded us to obey all these decrees and to fear the Lord our God, so that we might always prosper and be kept alive. If we are careful to obey all this law before the Lord our God, as he has commanded us, that will be our righteousness."[10]

Remembering Egypt also gave the Israelites motivation to obey God because they had seen with their own eyes how God brought one disaster after another on the land of Egypt. If they forsook the Lord and ceased to love and serve him, Moses warned them what would happen: "The Lord will send on you curses . . . until you are destroyed and come to sudden ruin because of the evil you have done in forsaking him. The Lord will plague you with diseases until he has destroyed you from the land you are entering to possess. . . . If you do not carefully follow all the words of this law, which are written in this book, and do not revere this glorious and awesome name—the Lord your God—the Lord will send fearful plagues on you and your descendants, harsh and prolonged disasters, severe and lingering illnesses." Moses warned that God would do the same to them as he had done to Egypt. "He will bring upon you all the diseases of Egypt that you dreaded, and they will cling to you. The Lord will also bring on you every kind of sickness and disaster not recorded in this book of the law, until you are destroyed . . . because you did not obey the Lord your God."[11] Egypt was a warning to them of what happened to a nation that despised the one true God.

Remembering Not to Fear

God's people were encamped on the border of Canaan and on the verge of war. They must remember their deliverance from Egypt so that they would not be afraid of the battles ahead of them. The Lord had fought for them in the past, releasing them from the power of Pharaoh and rescuing them from the army of Egypt—and that memory would help them to fight by faith rather than fleeing in fear. Moses repeated the words he had spoken to the Israelites when they had refused to fight their enemies forty years earlier: "Do not be terrified; do not be afraid of them. The Lord your God, who is going before you, will fight for you as he did for you in Egypt before your very eyes."[12] Later Moses said, "You may say to yourselves, 'These nations are stronger than we are. How can we drive them out?' But do not be afraid of them. Remember well what the Lord your God did to Pharaoh and to all Egypt. You saw with your own eyes the great trials, the miraculous signs and wonders, the mighty hand and outstretched arm, with which the Lord your God brought you out. The Lord your God will do the same to all the peoples you now fear. . . . Do not be terrified by them, for the Lord your God, who is among you, is a great and awesome God."[13]

Forty years earlier, when these soldiers of Israel were just little children, they had seen a terrifying sight with their own wide eyes: the whole army of Egypt pursuing them with horses and chariots. But they also had witnessed the Lord rescue them and their whole nation. God had drowned all their enemies in the Red Sea. Now Israel's soldiers who had seen these things in their childhood must bring these memories to mind and take courage from them. Even those who were too young to have seen this miracle must believe in God's deliverance, drawing strength and courage from hearing the story retold. Blessed were those who had not seen what God had done, yet believed it and recalled it, seeing God's deliverance with eyes of faith and remembering all that God had accomplished for them.

Remembering to be Compassionate

God's people must remember their deliverance from Egypt so that they would be compassionate towards other people. They had been slaves in Egypt, oppressed by a cruel and powerful nation. They must remember this and never become oppressors themselves, but instead follow God's example of granting justice and showing mercy to all. Moses said, "The Lord your God . . . shows no partiality and accepts no bribes. He defends the cause of the fatherless and the widow, and loves the alien, giving him food and clothing. And you are to love those who are aliens, for you yourselves were aliens in Egypt."[14] They must be like God, loving and helping those in need.[15]

God specifically instructed his people to pay careful attention that they were just and kind to the poor and to remember their poverty in Egypt. When the Israelites were harvesting the crops from their fields and gardens or gathering the fruit from their groves and vineyards, they were to leave some food behind for the poor people in their land who were struggling to survive. Moses commanded, "Leave what remains for the alien, the fatherless, and the widow. Remember that you were slaves in Egypt. That is why I command you to do this."[16]

If a fellow Israelite became so poor that he had to sell himself as a slave, he must be released after six years of service. Moses commanded, "In the seventh year you must let him go free. And when you release him, do not send him away empty-handed. Supply him liberally. . . . Give to him as the Lord your God has blessed you. Remember that you were slaves in Egypt and the Lord your God redeemed you. That is why I give you this command today."[17] They had experienced the Love of God, and now they must love other people, just as God had loved them. "We love, because he first loved us."[18]

Remembering That God Continues to Deliver His People

God's people must remember their deliverance from Egypt because it pointed them to the greater deliverance that God had planned from the beginning. The lesser deliverance—the clearly visible physical deliverance enacted here on earth—would help them to understand and accept the infinitely greater and invisible spiritual deliverance by which the Lord would bring them into heaven.[19] God performed this earthly salvation so that people might believe in the heavenly one.[20] It was still far in the future, but as surely as God had redeemed them from the power of Pharaoh's evil empire, so also God would save his people from the devil's dark power.[21] In their deliverance from Egypt, God clearly demonstrated to them and to the whole world that he was a saviour.

Remembering to Celebrate

It was so important for God's people to remember the deliverance from Egypt that the Lord instituted three celebrations to remind them continually of it: the Sabbath, celebrated every week; and the Passover and Firstfruits, celebrated at different times each year.

The Sabbath Day. The first celebration was the Sabbath Day. It was a day each week to honour the Lord, who was both their Creator and their Redeemer. His people were to rest on that day as a reminder that God had made them. "In six days the Lord created the heavens and the earth . . . but he rested on the seventh day. Therefore the Lord blessed the Sabbath Day and made it holy."[22] And just as God had rested from his labour, he gave his people rest from their ceaseless labour and hopeless bondage in Egypt. Now no one, not even a servant or slave, must work on that day. They all must observe the Sabbath by keeping it holy; they all must rest from their labours.[23] It was a weekly reminder that God, their redeemer, had set them free.

In Deuteronomy we see that the purpose of the Sabbath Day included redemption as well as creation. One day far in the future the Son of Man, who was Lord even of the Sabbath, would expand its purpose even further, changing that holy day of rest from the seventh day to the first day of the week— a day to remember his resurrection, and to celebrate the new creation and our full redemption in him.

The Passover. The second celebration of deliverance was the Passover, observed every year "on the anniversary of your departure from Egypt."[24] Connected with it was the Feast of Unleavened Bread, an annual seven-day festival which they were to celebrate "so that all the days of your life you may remember the time of your departure from Egypt."[25]

One day in the fullness of time, the Son of God would also change the Passover. It would be called the Lord's Supper, and it would help God's people to remember the greatest deliverance of all, when Jesus' body was broken and his blood poured out to purchase their freedom. No longer would they live their lives in bondage, chained and crushed by the weight of their guilt. No longer would they be under the power of Satan or ruled by the spiritual forces of evil at work in their hearts. Christ would set them free![26] Jesus offered himself as a sacrifice for our sins. "For Christ, our Passover Lamb, has been sacrificed."[27] When we celebrate the Passover meal, now called the Lord's Supper, Jesus our Saviour commanded us: "Do this in remembrance of me."[28]

The Firstfruits. The third celebration of the Israelites' deliverance from Egypt was the Firstfruits, and it was also observed each year. Moses gave Israel this command: "When you have entered the land the Lord your God is giving you . . . and have taken possession of it and have settled in it, then take some of the firstfruits of all that you produce from the soil of the land the Lord your God is giving you and put them in a basket. Then go to the place the Lord your God will choose as a dwelling for his name. The priest shall take the basket from your hands and set it down in front of the altar. . . . Then you shall declare before the Lord your God: 'My father[29] went down into Egypt with a few people and lived there and became a great nation, powerful and numerous. But the Egyptians mistreated us and made us suffer, putting us to hard labour. Then we cried out to the Lord, the God of our fathers, and the Lord heard our voice and saw our misery, toil and oppression. So the Lord brought us out of Egypt with a mighty hand and an outstretched arm, with great terror and with miraculous signs and wonders. He brought us to this place and gave us this land, a land flowing with milk and honey; and now I bring the firstfruits of the soil that you, O Lord, have given me.'"[30]

What an awesome sight that must have been, as thousands upon thousands of baskets of delicious fruits were set before the Lord's altar. What an awesome sound that must have been, as thousands upon thousands of people recited how God had saved them from their bondage in Egypt. Here before them was the proof that he had fulfilled his promise to set them free and to give them their own good and bountiful land. Then the people were to bow down and worship the Lord, rejoicing in the good things he had given them. Can you see the baskets of firstfruits—thousands upon thousands of them set before the altar—and hear the people declaring how God had saved them, singing and rejoicing in worship before the Lord?[31]

But that scene was a shadow on earth, pointing forward to another scene in heaven, where that celebration would reach its final fulfilment in Christ. Jesus was the beginning and firstborn of a new humanity; he was called the "firstfruits" of the great harvest of people in the resurrection.[32] Those who are united to Christ will be part of the new humanity,[33] raised to eternal life with Christ.[34] Now with the eyes of faith we can see and hear a great assembly, a countless multitude of people from every nation, tribe, people, and language, standing before the throne and in front of the Lamb of God. These people are the Israel of God, redeemed from the earth and purchased from among men, a new and resurrected humanity. They are offered as firstfruits to God and to the Lamb.[35] They are pure and undefiled; no lie is found in their mouths and they are blameless.[36] All together they declare the praises of the One who had saved them, crying out in a loud voice, "Salvation belongs to our God, who sits on the throne, and to the Lamb." And they sing a new song before the throne of the Lord.[37]

All of these celebrations reminded Israel of their time in Egypt; how they must honour and obey the Lord because of what he had done for them; and how he had set them free. But these celebrations also are pictures for us, enacted long ago, to point us to Christ. When we celebrate our Sabbath (the Lord's Day), and our Passover (the Lord's Supper), we too are remembering what God has done for us and how he has set us free. Let us look forward to that great day in heaven when together with all of those Christ has redeemed, we will sing and rejoice as we celebrate Jesus, our firstfruits and our Redeemer.

LESSON 2: TEACHER'S GUIDE

Do Not Forget: Remembering Egypt

VISUAL AIDS:

We have many ways of remembering important events in history: We set aside days; we have symbols and services; we take photos and write books; we paint pictures, make statues, write poems, and make movies; we collect souvenirs (from the French verb souvenir which means "to remember"); we set up museums—and so much more.

In Canada we celebrate Remembrance Day on November 11 each year to honour those who fought in World Wars I and 2. There is a symbol for that day—a red poppy, which everyone wears. Almost every community has an annual memorial service at a cenotaph, where the names of the soldiers who are buried overseas are listed. There are innumerable books and photos about the wars, along with favourite paintings and poems created by those who were soldiers during those years. Many families have souvenirs from the war. (My own family has a piece of shrapnel that wounded my grandfather; we also have his war medals and a huge brass World War I shell case.) You could bring many such items to class to show your children how a people can remember their history.

MEMORY WORK:

> "Remember your Creator in the days of your youth. . . . Remember him, before . . . the dust returns to the ground it came from, and the spirit returns to God who gave it."
>
> Ecclesiastes 12:1

REVIEW QUESTIONS:

1. Give several reasons why God wanted his people to remember their deliverance from Egypt.

2. What had he done to deliver them?
3. What special day each week and what special feasts each year helped the Israelites remember their deliverance from Egypt?
4. What celebrations has God given us to remember Christ's crucifixion and resurrection?
5. What has Christ done to deliver us?

PRAYER:

Our loving heavenly Father, we thank you for this precious history, which you have preserved for our sakes. When we are young and when we are old, may we always remember you and your great Love for us. We thank you for sending your Son Jesus to die on the cross to save us. May we never forget so great a salvation.

PSALMS TO SING:

These psalms speak of recalling God's works and never forgetting God's Word.

105A (1–3) . . . and 20A; 22EI; 42B; 77AB; 78A; 111A;
119B, G, K, L, O, S, U, W, X

Lesson 3

DO NOT FORGET

REMEMBERING THE DESERT

• Deuteronomy 5

After God's great deliverance of his people from Egypt, the Israelites still had many miles to travel, many years to live, and many lessons to learn before they would receive the promise and cross over into the land that God would give them. While they were in the desert, God revealed himself to his people at Mount Horeb, and he cared for them as they wandered in the wilderness. In spite of this, the people had continually rebelled. Moses reminded them of all these things as they prepared to enter the land, so that they would not forget the Lord their God, who had been faithful to them, even though they had not been faithful to worship and obey him.

Hearing God at Mount Horeb

A great period in Israel's history was the time they spent at the mountain of God, called Mount Horeb.[1] It was there that they heard the Lord's voice speak the Ten Commandments, and there he made his covenant with them. But the people were frightened by God's majesty and they asked Moses to go between them and the Lord.

Moses reminded the people, "The Lord our God made a covenant with us at Horeb. . . . The Lord spoke to you face to face out of the fire on the mountain. . . . When you heard the voice out of the darkness, while the mountain was ablaze with fire, all the leading men of your tribes and elders came to me. And you said, 'The Lord our God has shown us his glory and his majesty, and we have heard his voice from the fire. Today we have seen that a man can live even if God speaks with him. But now, why should we die? This great fire will consume us, and we will die if we hear the voice of the Lord our God any longer. For what mortal man has ever heard the voice of the living God speaking out of the fire, as we have, and survived? Go near and listen to all that the Lord our God says. Then tell us whatever the Lord our God tells you. We will listen and obey.'"[2]

Moses reminded the people how God had responded to their promise to obey: "Everything [my people] said was good. Oh, that their hearts would be inclined to fear me and keep all my commands always!" Moses told the people this story, asking them to remember the covenant they had made with the Lord, and how awesome and powerful he had shown himself to be at Mount Horeb.

What happened at Mount Horeb was another crucial event that would remind the Israelites of God's power and might. Not only did he deliver them from Egypt, but he spoke directly to them from a mountain covered with smoke and fire. They must remember what happened at Horeb so they would know that the Lord is God. Moses said, "Ask now about the former days, long before your time, from the day God created man on the earth; ask from one end of the heavens to the other. Has anything so great as this ever happened or has anything like it ever been heard of? Has any other people heard the voice of God speaking out of fire, as you have, and lived? You were shown these things so that you might know that the Lord is God; besides him there is no other. . . . Acknowledge and take to heart this day that the Lord is God in heaven above and on earth below. There is no other."[3]

They must remember what happened at Horeb to keep themselves from worshipping images or idols. Did they see the Lord their God? Did their eyes behold any form? No. They only heard his voice. Therefore they must never make a visible representation of God. Moses warned the people, "Be careful and watch yourselves closely so that you do not forget the things your eyes have seen or let them slip from your heart as long as you live. Teach them to your children and to their children after them. Remember the day you stood before the Lord your God at Horeb. . . . You saw no form of any kind the day the Lord spoke to you at Horeb out of the fire. Therefore, watch yourselves carefully, so that you do not become corrupt and make for yourselves an idol, an image of any shape, whether formed like a man or a woman or like any animal on earth. . . . Be careful; do not forget the covenant of the Lord your God that he made with you. Do not make for yourselves an idol in the form of anything. . . . For the Lord your God is a consuming fire."[4]

They must remember what happened at Horeb because it was a clear demonstration of God's Love for them. When Moses, the man of God, blessed the Israelites before his death, he said, "Surely it is you [O Lord], who love the people; all the holy ones are in your hand. At your feet they all bow down, and from you they receive instruction, the law that Moses gave us, the possession of the assembly of Jacob."[5] God's gift of his law to Israel and the awesome manner in which it was given were signs of his great Love for his people. Israel possessed a great national treasure—the commandments of God![6]

The Israelites had a constant reminder of that great day at the foot of Mount Horeb: the two stone tablets that were safely stored in the ark of the covenant. The Lord had given the tablets, inscribed with his commandments, to Moses on that awesome day at the foot of the mountain.[7] The memory of this day was to be planted forever in the hearts of all who witnessed it and then transplanted into the minds of all who came after it, so that the Lord and his laws—inscribed on tablets of stone as a constant reminder for the Israelites—would be honoured and obeyed forever.

Wandering in the Desert

The Israelites' long journey through "that vast and dreadful desert"[8] was another part of their history that they must not forget. The Lord led them "through the barren wilderness, through a land of deserts and rifts, through a land of drought and darkness and the shadow of death, through a land where no one travels and no one lives"[9]—a land that could not support life. Yet the Lord sustained an entire nation in that perilous place.

During forty hard years of wandering, God guided them and guarded them and granted them everything they needed to live.

In Deuteronomy, Moses reminded the people of what he had said to them the last time they were camped on the edge of the Promised Land. At that time he had urged them not to be afraid, telling them, "The Lord your God, who is going before you, will fight for you, as he did for you . . . in the desert. There you saw how the Lord your God carried you, as a father carries his son, all the way you went until you reached this place."[10] Moses exhorted the people: "Remember how the Lord your God led you all the way in the desert these forty years."[11] God went ahead of them on their journey, in fire by night and in a cloud by day, to search out places for them to camp and to show them the way they must go.[12] They must take courage from remembering that the Lord himself carried them through the wilderness. If the Lord had cared for them as they wandered in the desert, surely he could care for them—guiding, guarding, and providing—as they entered this land of abundance.

Moses reminded the people of how God had led them safely through a harsh land. He told them, "The Lord your God has blessed you . . . and has watched over your journey through this vast desert."[13] In his song at the end of this book, Moses taught the people, "In a desert land God found Israel, in a barren and howling waste. [The Lord] shielded him and cared for him; he guarded him as the apple of his eye, like an eagle that stirs up its nest and hovers over its young, that spreads its wings to catch them and carries them on its pinions. The Lord alone led him."[14]

Moses also reminded the people of the enemies they had faced on that journey and the victories they had won along the way. Israel had defeated two wicked kings, destroyed their strong armies, and conquered their vast kingdoms. How had they accomplished all this? Moses said, "The Lord our God gave us all of them."[15] Moses commanded Joshua, the man who would soon become Israel's new leader, "You have seen with your own eyes all that the Lord your God has done to these two kings. The Lord will do the same to all the kingdoms over there where you are going. Do not be afraid of them. The Lord your God himself will fight for you"[16]—just as he had done for them in the past.

Moses continued on to tell the Israelites of the Lord's goodness to them, reminding them that the Lord had provided everything necessary for life while they wandered in that desolate wasteland. Throughout their journey in that barren region, God miraculously provided food and water for the whole nation. "These forty years the Lord your God has been with you, and you have not lacked anything,"[17] Moses said. "God led you through the vast and dreadful desert, that thirsty and waterless land, with its venomous snakes and scorpions. He brought you water out of hard rock. He gave you manna to eat in the desert. . . . Remember the Lord your God."[18] Moses also reminded the people that their clothes and shoes did not wear out during those forty long years.[19] All the time they wandered in the wilderness, God had provided for their physical needs. From the soles of their tired feet, which did not swell on that forty-year journey, to the hairs upon their weary heads, which were all numbered, the Lord was taking care of his people.[20]

In the desert God also provided for the spiritual needs of his people. The Lord was training them to live by faith—to rely upon him and his word. Moses said, "Remember how the Lord your God led you all the way in the desert these forty years, to humble you and to test you in order to know what was in your heart, whether or not you would keep his commands. He humbled you, causing you to hunger and then feeding you with manna . . . to teach you that man does not live on bread alone, but on every Word that comes from the mouth of the Lord. . . . Know then in your heart, that as a man disciplines his son, so the Lord your God disciplines you."[21] This too was a sign of God's Love, "because the Lord disciplines those he loves," just as a father disciplines the child in whom he takes delight,[22] taking the time to train that child. Because God loved Israel, he trained and tested them in the wilderness.

Celebrating the Desert

The Lord instituted a yearly celebration to remind the people of their time in the wilderness, when they wandered from place to place, living in make-shift shelters and eating the manna which lay upon the ground. In the wilderness the people had no homes to shelter them and no fields for growing food. They owned nothing in that barren wilderness, yet God provided for them.

To remember their time in the desert, God commanded that every year for seven days they must celebrate the Lord's Feast of Tabernacles. On the first day of this festival they were to gather choice fruit and leafy branches from the trees in the good land the Lord had given them, and with these they were to build little shelters for themselves. They were to live in these "tabernacles" for seven days to remind them of the humble way they lived in the wilderness. They would see the choice fruit hanging from the branches of their shelters and they would remember the forty years in the wilderness when they had no fruit to eat.[23] The head of each family was to bring an offering for the feast, "a gift in proportion to the way the Lord your God has blessed you."[24] Moses said "Celebrate the Feast of Tabernacles for seven days. . . . Be joyful at your feast. . . . For the Lord your God will bless you in all your harvest and in all the work of your hands, and your joy will be complete."[25]

The People's Rebellion

The people must always remember who God was and all that he had done for them, but they also must remember who they were and all that they had done. In gratitude for God's Love and care, had they served and loved the Lord their God with heart, soul, and strength? Had they honoured the Lord and worshipped him with joy and thanksgiving? Had they delighted in God's teaching, accepting his discipline and learning from their mistakes? Sadly, they had not adored the Lord or devoted their lives to him; they had not even believed or obeyed him. Deuteronomy is a book that reminds the Israelites of their many failures and constant rebellion against God.

The book of Deuteronomy opens with Moses reminding the people that almost forty years earlier God had brought them to very edge of the Promised Land, just as they were now. But they had rebelled against God. Moses told them of their failure to believe that God would give them victory against their enemies: "You were unwilling to go up; you rebelled against the command of the Lord your God. You grumbled in your tents. . . . You did not trust in the Lord your God. . . . You rebelled against the Lord's command."[26] Again Moses reminded the people that when God commanded them to take possession of the land he had promised to give them, they rebelled. "You rebelled against the command of the Lord your God. You did not trust him or obey him. You have been rebellious against the Lord ever since I have known you!"[27] What was the consequence of this rebellion? God solemnly swore, "Not a man of this evil generation shall see the good land"[28]—and they all died in the desert, just as the Lord had said.

The Israelites had also rebelled at Mount Horeb. While Moses was on the mountain, receiving the two stone tablets of the covenant, the Israelites had sinned against the Lord by making and worshipping an idol cast in the shape of a calf. When Moses came down from the mountain and saw what they had done, he took the stone tablets, threw them out of his hands, and broke them into pieces before their eyes. Moses took that sinful thing they had made, that stupid golden calf which they called their god, and he burned their idol in the fire. Then he crushed it, ground it into powder, threw it into the stream, and made them drink it. Moses said, "Remember this and never forget how you provoked the Lord your God to anger in the desert. Until the day you left Egypt until you arrived here, you have been rebellious against the Lord. At Horeb you aroused the Lord's wrath so that he was angry enough to destroy you."[29]

Refusing to follow the Lord into battle and creating an idol—a golden image of a calf!—to replace him were two very significant occasions of disobedience in Israel's history. But these were certainly not the only times God's people turned away from him. Moses reminded the Israelites of other rebellions in the wilderness and the terrifying consequences of them. They saw with their own eyes what God did to the rebels, how "the earth opened its mouth right in the middle of all Israel and swallowed them up," how thousands of them were destroyed by a plague for immorality and idolatry, how fire from the Lord burned among them because they provoked the Lord to wrath with their complaining.[30] These were terrifying judgements, which Moses did not want them to forget.

But wouldn't it be better to put these awful memories behind them? No, Moses wanted God's people to remember these horrifying events as warnings not to rebel against the Lord. It was better to be afraid of God than to be destroyed because of continual rebellion against him. Their history was a warning to them to be on guard against themselves and against the sin which so easily entangled them.

God's Reminder to Us

These events that Moses reviewed in Deuteronomy were not only important for the Israelites to remember—Deuteronomy is God's Word for us as well. Our faith also will be strengthened as we recall all God's miracles, and we will be encouraged to depend on the Lord to save us. We will be helped to trust and hope in God as we remember Israel's deliverance from Egypt, God's voice at Mount Horeb, and the journey through the wilderness.

Israel's history is also a warning for us. We read in the New Testament, "Now these things occurred as examples to keep us from setting our hearts on evil things, as they did. Do not be idolaters, as some of them were. . . . We should not commit sexual immorality, as some of them did—and in one day 23,000 of them died. We should not test the Lord, as some of them did—and were killed by snakes. And do not grumble, as some of them did—and were killed by the destroying angel. These things happened to them as examples and were written down as warnings for us, on whom the fulfilment of the ages has come."[31]

We too must always remember. We too must never forget. To help us, God has sent his Holy Spirit, who will not only comfort us and instruct us, but will also remind us of all that is written in the Scriptures—from the words of Moses to the words of the One greater than Moses. Jesus said, "The Counsellor, the Holy Spirit, whom the Father will send in my name, will teach you all things and will remind you of everything I have said to you."[32] We too must resolve to remember all that God has said and done.

> I will remember the deeds of the Lord.
> Yes, I will remember your miracles of long ago.
> I will meditate on all your works
> and consider all your mighty deeds.
>
> —Psalm 77:11–12

LESSON 3: TEACHER'S GUIDE

Do Not Forget: Remembering the Desert

VISUAL AIDS:

See visual aids for lesson 2; you could also find photographs of stone tablets like the ones the Lord wrote on when he gave Moses the Ten Commandments, or of the booths used in the Feast of Tabernacles.

MEMORY WORK:

"I will remember the deeds of the Lord. Yes, I will remember your miracles of long ago."

Psalm 77:11

"This is what the Lord says: 'Remember this. Fix it in mind. Take it to heart, you rebels. Remember the former things, those of long ago. I am God, and there is no other; I am God, and there is none like me.'"

Isaiah 46:8–9

REVIEW QUESTIONS:

1. In Deuteronomy, Moses reviews Israel's history. What main events in their history did Moses recall repeatedly in this book?
2. Give several reasons why God wanted his people to remember their time at Mount Horeb.
3. What did the Israelites have to remind them of their time at the mountain?
4. Give several reasons why God wanted his people to remember the journey in the desert.

5. What yearly celebration helped them to remember their wanderings in the wilderness?
6. Moses reminded the people of all the awesome things that God had done for his people. Moses also reminded them of what they had done. What had the people done continually? How did God punish them?
7. Why did Moses want the people to remember these terrifying events?
8. Why is it important for us to remember these events as well?
9. Whom has God sent as a Counsellor, to help us remember?

PRAYER:

Lord, we thank you for your merciful and bountiful care of us. Day after day, throughout our whole lives, you provide for us in every way. We thank you also for the Holy Spirit, who comforts us and reminds us of the truth. Forgive us, that we are not always mindful or thankful or joyful of our many blessings.

PSALMS TO SING:

See the psalms for Lesson 2, which speak of remembering all God's mighty deeds.

Lesson 4

THE SECRET OF SUCCESS

• Deuteronomy 11:1–25

Soon Israel would be marching into the Promised Land—but when that finally came to pass, Moses would no longer be with them. Before his soldiers advanced into enemy territory, Moses wanted to give them a secret weapon to ensure their victory. He did not divulge a radical military strategy or unveil some strange new artillery—no, the secret to their success could be summarised in a single word: obedience.

Moses said, "Hear now, O Israel, the decrees and laws I am about to teach you. Follow them so that you may live and may go in and take possession of the land that the Lord, the God of your fathers, is giving you."[1] Later in the book, Moses reminded them, "If you carefully observe all these commands I am giving you to follow—to love the Lord your God, to walk in all his ways and to hold fast to him—then the Lord will drive out all these nations before you and you will dispossess nations larger and stronger than you. Every place where you set your foot will be yours. . . . No man will be able to stand against you."[2] The secret of their success in conquering the land was obedience to the law of the Lord their God.

But the Israelites could not just do as they pleased once the Lord had defeated their enemies. No, obedience was also the secret of success if the Israelites desired to remain in the land and prosper there. From beginning to end in the book of Deuteronomy, Moses declared to Israel the necessity of obeying the commands of God. That was the only way their lives would continue to be blessed. Moses said, "Acknowledge and take to heart this day that the Lord is God in heaven above and on the earth below. There is no other. Keep his decrees and commands, which I am giving you today, so that it may go well with you and your children after you and that you may live long in the land the Lord your God gives you for all time."[3]

The Lord longed for his people to follow him so that he could bless them. Moses reminded the people what God said when he made his covenant with them at Mount Horeb: "Oh, that their hearts would be inclined to fear me and keep all my commands always, so that it might go well with them and their children forever!"[4] So Moses urged the people, "Be careful to do what the Lord your God has commanded you. Do not turn aside to the right or to the left. Walk in all the way that the Lord your God has commanded you, so that you may live and prosper and prolong your days in the land you will possess."[5]

The very last words that Moses spoke to the Israelites, just before he pronounced his final benediction, were to urge them again to obey the Lord. Moses' final exhortation to his flock was this: "Take to heart all the words I have solemnly declared to you this day, so that you may command your children to obey carefully all the words of this law. They are not just idle words for you—they are your life. By them you will live long in the land you are crossing the Jordan to possess."[6]

Success in the Eyes of the Nations

Not only would the Israelites increase and prosper by following the Lord, but their obedience would make them a great nation. Moses said, "If you fully obey the Lord your God and carefully follow all his commands I give you today, the Lord your God will set you high above all the nations on earth. All these blessings will come upon you and accompany you if you obey the Lord your God."[7] The countries surrounding them would recognize their greatness—and the greatness of the Lord their God. Moses said, "See, I have taught you decrees and laws, as the Lord my God commanded me. . . . Observe them carefully, for this will show your wisdom and understanding to the nations, who will hear about all these laws and say, 'Surely this great nation is a wise and understanding people.' What other nation is so great, as to have their gods near them the way the Lord our God is near us whenever we pray to him? And what other nation is so great as to have such righteous decrees and laws as this body of laws I am setting before you today? Only be careful and watch yourselves closely."[8]

Moses told the people that if they followed the Lord, he would send a blessing on everything that they attempted to do—and the nations would notice. "The Lord your God will bless you in the land he is giving you. The Lord will establish you as his holy people, as he promised you on oath—if you keep the commands of the Lord your God and walk in his ways. Then all the peoples on earth will see that you are called by the name of the Lord, and they will fear you. If you pay attention to the commands of the Lord your God that I give you this day and carefully follow them, you will always be at the top, never at the bottom."[9] It wasn't enough to have these laws and know these laws; their success as a nation depended upon observing and enforcing these laws. Then the whole world would acknowledge their greatness.

Success for Future Generations

The Lord promised the Israelites victory and greatness if they obeyed him as they entered the Promised Land, but they must continue to obey if they wanted to remain there—if they wanted to settle there and prosper there; if they wanted to keep their homes and farms and towns in the Promised Land; if they wanted this land to belong to the generations after them; if they wanted their descendants to live there and be blessed also. They must be careful to obey and pass on all God's laws so that their children and grandchildren and great-grandchildren after them would remain in the land too.

Moses said to them, "These are the commands, decrees, and laws the Lord your God directed me to teach you to observe in the land that you are crossing the Jordan to possess, so that you, your children, and their children after them may fear the Lord your God as long as you live by keeping all his decrees and commands that I give you, and so that you may enjoy long life. These commandments that I give you today are to be upon your hearts. Impress them on your children. Talk about them when you sit at home and when you walk along the road, when you lie down and when you get up. Tie them as symbols on your hands and bind them on your foreheads. Write them on the doorframes of your houses and on your gates."[10]

And when the Israelite children asked the meaning of all these laws, their parents were to explain how the Lord had rescued them, bringing them out of the land of slavery and into the land of promise. Then they were to tell the children, "The Lord commanded us to obey all these decrees and to fear the Lord our God, so that we might always prosper and be kept alive, as is the case today. And if we are careful to obey all this law before the Lord our God, as he has commanded us, that will be our righteousness."[11] What a great nation they would be! Not only would they have long life and a good land if they continued to follow the Lord, they would have righteousness too.

Guarding Against Idolatry

They must especially be on the alert lest they and their children slip and fall into the sin of idolatry. They had disobeyed God's law and broken God's covenant by committing this sin of idolatry in the wilderness, and God had almost destroyed them. They had been surrounded by the worship of idols and false gods in Egypt, the land from which they had come, and they would be faced with that same temptation in Canaan, the land to which they were going. Therefore Moses warned them, "Watch yourselves very carefully, so that you do not become corrupt and make for yourselves an idol, an image of any shape. And when you look up to the sky and see the sun, the moon, and the stars—all the heavenly array—do not be enticed into bowing down to them."[12]

Moses reminded them, "Be careful not to forget the covenant of the Lord your God that he made with you. Do not make for yourselves an idol in the form of anything. After you have had children and grandchildren and have lived in the land a long time—if you then become corrupt and make any kind of idol, doing evil in the eyes of the Lord your God and provoking him to anger, I call heaven and earth as witnesses against you this day, that you will quickly perish from the land that you are crossing the Jordan to possess. you will not live there long, but will certainly be destroyed! The Lord will scatter you among the peoples, and only a few of you will survive among the nations to which the Lord will drive you."[13]

The people of God must worship God according to all his commands, which carefully regulated all their feasts and sacrifices. They must not imitate the worship of the nations around them, but "observe everything I command you," said Moses. "Be careful to obey all these regulations I am giving you, so that it may always go well with you and your children after you, because you will be doing what is good and right in the eyes of the Lord your God. See that you do all I command you; do not add to it or take away from it."[14]

As surely as God brought them into the Promised Land, he would drive them out again if they were not faithful to follow only the Lord. They must obey and worship God as he had commanded them—their survival as a nation depended upon it.

Remaining Faithful in Times of Prosperity

Moses warned the people not to forget God in the days of prosperity that were coming. He exhorted them, "Observe the commands of the Lord your God, walking in his ways and revering him. For the Lord your God is bringing you into a good land, ... a land where bread will not be scarce and you will lack nothing. . . . When you have eaten and are satisfied, praise the Lord your God for the good land he has given you. Be careful that you do not forget the Lord your God, failing to observe his commands, his laws, and his decrees that I am giving you this day. Otherwise when you eat and are satisfied, when you build fine houses and settle down, and when your herds and flocks grow large and your silver and gold increase and all you have is multiplied, then your heart will become proud and you will forget the Lord your God, who brought you out of Egypt, out of the land of slavery. You may say to yourself, 'My power and the strength of my hands have produced this wealth for me.' But remember the Lord your God, for it is he who gives you the ability to produce wealth, and so confirms his covenant, which he swore to your forefathers, as it is today. If you ever forget the Lord your God and follow other gods and worship and bow down to them, I testify against you today, that you will surely be destroyed.

Like the nations the Lord destroyed before you, so you will be destroyed for not obeying the Lord your God."[15]

Again Moses reminded them, "When the Lord your God brings you into the land he swore to your fathers to Abraham, Isaac and Jacob to give you—a land with large flourishing cities you did not build, houses filled with all kinds of good things you did not provide, wells you did not dig, and vineyards and olive groves you did not plant—then when you eat and are satisfied, be careful that you do not forget the Lord. . . . Fear the Lord your God. Serve him only. . . . Do not follow other gods, the gods of the peoples around you; for the Lord your God, who is among you, is a jealous God and his anger will burn against you, and he will destroy you from the face of the land. Do not test the Lord your God. . . . Do what is right and good in the Lord's sight, so that it may go well with you and you may go in and take over the good land that the Lord promised on oath to your forefathers, thrusting out all your enemies before you, as the Lord said."[16]

Success in Tending the Land

Moses explained to the Israelites that Canaan was not like Egypt, where the crops had to be irrigated with water from the Nile. No, the Promised Land was watered by the Lord, who sent rain from heaven. Moses said, "It is a land the Lord your God cares for; the eyes of the Lord your God are continually on it from the beginning of the year to its end."[17] So if the people faithfully obeyed the Lord's commands—loving the Lord and serving him with all their heart and all their soul—then God would send rain on the land at the right time and in the proper season, so that their farms and fields and crops, their flocks and herds, and all they had would flourish. "But," Moses warned, "be careful, or you will be enticed to turn away and worship other gods and bow down to them. Then the Lord's anger will burn against you, and he will shut the heavens, so that it will not rain and the ground will yield no produce, and you will soon perish from the good land that the Lord your God is giving you."[18]

A Covenant for Their Good

At the end of Moses' words to the Israelites, he and all the people renewed their covenant with the Lord. At that time, Moses again urged the people to be obedient. He said, "Carefully follow the terms of this covenant, so that you may prosper in everything you do."[19] What were the terms of the covenant? That Israel would follow the law of the Lord, that he in turn would give them fame and honour among the nations, and that they would be his people, his treasured possession, a people holy to the Lord.

Moses said to them, "The Lord your God commands you this day to follow these decrees and laws; carefully observe them with all your heart and with all your soul. You have declared this day that the Lord is your God and that you will walk in his ways, that you will keep his decrees, commands and laws, and that you will obey him. And the Lord has declared this day that you are his people, his treasured possession as he promised, and that you are to keep all his commands. He has declared that he will set you in praise, fame and honour high above all the nations he has made and that you will be a people holy to the Lord your God, as he promised."[20]

This was not to be a burdensome covenant for the people—the Lord had given them himself and his law for their own good! Moses made this clear when he asked the Israelites this question: "And now, O Israel, what does the Lord your God ask of you, but to fear the Lord your God, to walk in all his ways, to love him, to serve the Lord your God with all your heart and with all your soul, and to observe the Lord's commands and decrees that I am giving you today for your own good?"[21] This was the Lord's covenant of Love with them, so that they might have success, and so the Lord might bless them. Moses commanded the Israelites, "Take care to follow the commands, decrees, and laws I give you today. If you pay attention to these laws and are careful to follow them, then the Lord your God will keep his covenant of Love with you, as he swore to your forefathers. He will love you and bless you and increase your numbers. He will bless the fruit of your womb, [and] the crops of your land. . . . You will be blessed more than any other people."[22]

Doomed to Failure

From beginning to end in the book of Deuteronomy, Moses stressed the necessity of obedience to the laws of God. He urged the people to obey the commands of the Lord for their own good, so that they would be blessed in everything. To conquer the land, to survive in the land, to prosper in the land, they must obey God. To be praised and feared as a great nation in the world, they must obey God. That was the key to their success—the key which would unlock the storehouse of all God's blessings—and the greatest blessing was that they would be God's people, holy to the Lord. All the Israelites had to do was obey his covenant as revealed in the Ten Commandments, and God himself would bless them in every way. The secret was so simple. Success seemed so certain. As Moses himself said, "What I am commanding you today is not too difficult for you or beyond your reach."[23]

But alas, God knew that Israel would fail, breaking his covenant. He said, "These people will soon prostitute themselves to the foreign gods of the land they are entering. They will forsake me and break the covenant I made with them. On that day I will become angry with them and forsake them; I will hide my face from them and they will be destroyed. . . . because of all their wickedness in turning to other gods. When I have brought them into the land flowing with milk and honey, the land I promised on oath to their forefathers,. . . . they will turn to other gods and worship them, rejecting me and breaking my covenant. . . . I know what they are disposed to do, even before I bring them into the land I promised them."[24]

Moses also knew that the people would rebel against the Lord, grievously disobeying all his commandments. Before they ever entered the Promised Land, Moses prophesied Israel's failure, telling them, "I know how rebellious and stiff-necked you are. If you have been rebellious against the Lord while I am still alive and with you, how much more will you rebel after I die! For I know that after my death you are sure to become utterly corrupt and to turn from the way that I have commanded you. In days to come, disaster will fall upon you because you will do evil in the sight of the Lord and provoke him to anger by what your hands have made."[25] And it was true that in the future Israel would return to the worship of idols that they made with their own hands. They would break God's covenant and disobey all God's commandments.

Hearts Inclined to Rebellion

Why would Israel fail, continuing to rebel against God? They had so much to gain by obedience, by honouring and cherishing the covenant, and so much to lose by disobedience. Why wouldn't they just do what was right?

The problem with Israel was the same one that afflicted the entire human race. The problem was within human nature itself—the hardness of the human heart. Although "God made mankind upright,"[26] the universal condition of our hearts quickly became "deceitful and desperately wicked."[27] Even in the early days of mankind, when God looked down from heaven, "the Lord saw how great man's wickedness on the earth had become and that every inclination of the thoughts of his heart was only evil all the time. The [whole] earth was corrupt in God's sight and was full of violence."[28]

The Scripture declares that the whole world is a prisoner of sin.[29] All people stand condemned before God because all have sinned.[30] The Israelites promised to keep God's law in order to have life, but they were no different from the rest of the human race. Even the people chosen by God could not perfectly keep those righteous laws so graciously revealed to them, in which they had the embodiment of truth and knowledge. "If a law had been given that could impart life, then righteousness would certainly have come by the law"[31]—but that perfect law given to Israel was something they were incapable of keeping. Since the day sin entered the world, the hearts of all human beings naturally and relentlessly have inclined towards rebellion and destruction, and the Israelites were no exception. God said Israel was "a rebellious nation that has rebelled against me. They and their fathers have been in revolt against me to this very day."[32] He described them over and over as "a rebellious house."[33] In this the Israelites were no different from the rest of mankind. The whole world is in rebellion against God.[34]

Moses himself made it very clear to the Israelites that God did not choose them to receive the Promised Land because of their inherent goodness. "No," Moses said, "it is because of the wickedness of these nations that the Lord is driving them out before you. It is not because of your righteousness or the uprightness of your heart that you go in to possess their land, but because of the wickedness of these nations. . . . Understand, then, that it is not because of your righteousness. . . . for you are a stiff-necked people."[35] But although they were not naturally more righteous than other peoples, Israel did have something which no other nation on earth had at that time: "They were entrusted with the very words of God."[36]

The Purpose of the Law

But what good was the law to them, if they were unable to keep the covenant by obeying God's commandments? Why did God bother to reveal to Israel this "secret of success," if it was all so pointless and hopeless? It almost seems like the command to obey God's law was more a formula for failure than a secret of success—asking the Israelites to do the impossible, and then condemning them for breaking the law when they could not do otherwise, since they were simply acting in accordance with their sinful nature. If God's law could not, in fact, impart life, was God just teasing these morally retarded and corrupted human beings with a standard of perfection that they were utterly incapable of attaining? Was God's law a trap, designed to ensnare and destroy all people?

Nothing could be farther from the truth! God is Love and the giving of his holy law was an act of his grace—it was called a covenant of Love. It was not given to ensnare us. "'As surely as I live,' declares the Sovereign LORD, 'I take no pleasure in the death of the wicked, but rather that they turn from their ways and live.'"[37]

God had a great and glorious purpose for his people in the giving of his law. We read in the Scriptures that "the law is holy and the commandment is holy, righteous, and good."[38] The problem was not with God's law; the problem was that humans beings were not holy, not righteous, not good; they were the ones who were not spiritual or perfect. That was one reason God gave us his law—to show us how wretchedly far our race had fallen from a state of moral and spiritual perfection. Since our entire subjective human experience would be as sinful beings involved with other sinful human beings, how could we possibly know that we were defective creatures, unless there was revealed to us an objective standard of spiritual measurement? Thanks be to God, "through the law we become conscious of sin." Indeed, we would not have known what sin was except through the law.[39]

It was all part of God's plan. It was God's purpose in the old covenant with Israel to show all people the true desperation of the human condition. We are all rebels at heart. Before Christ works in us, we are alienated from God by our sins, enemies of God in the depths of our souls, and dead in our sins. Destruction is all that we can earn for ourselves, for our wicked hearts constantly betray us, and we are unable to keep ourselves from the corruption of sin and death working within us. Evil is always there, living within us and waging war against the holy law of God. The devil—with all the demonic powers of darkness and the spiritual forces of wickedness in the invisible realms—holds us captive, chaining us in our own sinful souls, trapping us in our own bodies of death. The law could not set us free. Scripture says "we were held prisoners by the law."[40] Nor could God's law grant us life—it could only show us our wretched condition and prove that we deserved the condemnation we dreaded.

That was what God, in his great Love for us, designed the law to do, so that we would be forced to turn to him and cry out from the depths of our souls, "God, have mercy on me, a sinner! Oh wretched person that I am! Who will rescue me from this body of death?"[41] He gave us his law to drive us to our knees and lead us to Christ.[42] That is how the law would revive our souls—by leading us to the one who is Life, who by his death brought life to the world. The law brought judgment and death, but what the law of God could not do—impart life—the Son of God did.[43]

Jesus said, "Everyone who looks to the Son and believes in him shall have eternal life, and I will raise him up at the last day. . . . I tell you the truth, he who believes has everlasting life."[44] Again Jesus declared, "I am the resurrection and the life. He who believes in me will live, even though he dies; and whoever lives and believes in me will never die. Do you believe this?"[45]

Dear children, do you believe this? "Behold how great is the Love that God has lavished upon us,"[46] that he has made a way for us to live with him forever. Faith in Jesus Christ—that is the true secret of success!

LESSON 4: TEACHER'S GUIDE

The Secret of Success

VISUAL AIDS:

Show your young Bible students two large old keys on a single key ring or chain. The twin keys to Israel's success were believing God and obeying God. The door to success could not be opened or unlocked without these two keys.

MEMORY WORK:

"Love the Lord your God and keep his laws and his commands always."
Deuteronomy 11:1

"What does the Lord your God ask of you, but to fear the Lord your God, to walk in all his ways, to love him, to serve the Lord your God with all your heart and with all your soul, and to observe the Lord's commands. . . . for your own good?"
Deuteronomy 10:12–13

"Jesus said, 'If you love me, keep my commandments.'"
John 14:15

REVIEW QUESTIONS:

1. Repeatedly in Deuteronomy Moses told the Israelites the secret to success in battle as they fought for the Promised Land. What was this secret?
2. Believing and obeying the Lord would ensure their victory in the war. What would ensure their prosperity once they settled in the Promised Land?
3. Israel could be a great nation, admired by all the surrounding nations. What must they do to be that great nation?

4. Parents are concerned for their children and their grandchildren and their great-grandchildren. What must the Israelites do to keep them all safely in the Promised Land?
5. The Israelites must be constantly alert, lest they fall into a terrible sin which would surely destroy them. What was that sin?
6. Why did this sin so easily ensnare them? What would happen to them in the Promised Land if they slipped into this sin again?
7. Moses gave the Israelites the secret to success. It was so simple. Would Israel succeed?
8. Why would Israel fail to keep God's commandments?
9. The Bible says that "the whole world is a prisoner of sin."[47] How can we escape? Who can set us free?
10. God had a great and glorious purpose in the giving of his law. What was this purpose?

PRAYER:

O Lord, our loving heavenly Father, we thank you for your holy law. Help us to love you and serve you and keep your commandments. We praise you for our Saviour, Jesus Christ, who died to release us from the power of sin and the penalty of your law. O Lord, we can never thank you enough for sending your blessed Son into this world to save us. Thank you for your great Love for us!

PSALMS TO SING:

25C. This psalm speaks of the "secret of the Lord," which is the knowledge of his covenant—the Ten Commandments. However, we rely upon God's mercy to save us as we entreat him "to pardon my iniquity, for it is very great."

These are just a few of the many psalms which praise God for his kindness and speak of our desperate need for his mercy, even while we strive to know and to keep God's commandments:

143C . . . and 36B; 57B (1, 9, 10); 67A; 78D; 85A; 86A;
98B (1–3); 100ABC; 103A; 116A; 119HQR; 130AB; 138AB

Lesson 5

THE TEN COMMANDMENTS . . . AGAIN

- Deuteronomy 5–6
- Matthew 22:34–40
- Mark 12:28–34

Moses gave the Ten Commandments to Israel twice. The first time was just after leaving Egypt; this second time was just before entering Canaan. The name "Deuteronomy" comes from this second law-giving. It is made up of two Greek words: *deuteros* (second) and *nomos* (law). God did not give them a second set of laws—he gave the same ten commandments to Israel a second time.

The first time the Israelites heard the law of the Lord proclaimed, God spoke to them out of the fire and cloud and deep darkness on Mount Horeb. What a privilege to hear the voice of God speak the law of God! The second time the Israelites heard the law of the Lord, it was proclaimed to them by the voice of Moses on the banks of the Jordan River, as he gave his final words to the people. That generation too was blessed, because they heard the voice of Moses speak the Ten Commandments. There was only one generation of Jews who would be more privileged: those who heard the voice of the Messiah, the Son of God, proclaim God's holy and perfect law when he taught in the land of Israel.[1]

When the Israelites were camped on the eastern side of the Jordan River across from the Promised Land, Moses summoned all Israel and said, "Hear O Israel the decrees and laws I declare in your hearing today. Learn them and be sure to follow them." Moses told them it was the same law and the same covenant that the Lord made with them at Mount Horeb years before, and then he repeated the Ten Commandments to them almost word for word. Throughout the book of Deuteronomy, he enlarged upon these commandments and how they must be applied and enforced once the people arrived in the Promised Land.

The Commandments About Loving God

The first four commandments deal with loving the Lord. Once Jesus was asked, "Out of all the commandments in the law, which is the greatest?" He answered by quoting Deuteronomy: "Hear O Israel, the Lord is our God, the Lord alone! Love the Lord your God with all your heart and with all your soul and with all your mind and with all your strength." Jesus declared, "This is the first and greatest commandment."[2] All the laws about loving and worshipping God can be summed up in that one command.

1. You shall have no other gods before me.
2. You shall not make for yourself an idol in the form of anything. . . .You shall not bow down to them or worship them.
3. You shall not misuse the name of the lord your God.
4. Observe the Sabbath day by keeping it holy.

When the Israelites entered Canaan, they were entering a land filled with idols and idol-worshippers who did not love the Lord. The land was utterly polluted with false gods and wicked practices. There were idols on every hill, under every tree, inside every house. Although the Promised Land was a good land, flowing with milk and honey, it was also a land overflowing with evil because of the wicked nations who possessed the land at that time. Their sin had reached its full measure and God would tolerate it no longer.[3] There were many things which the Israelites must do to make the land a holy dwelling place for the Lord their God, where he would be loved and honoured according to the first four commands.

In order to clear the Promised Land of idol worship, the Israelites must first destroy the wicked nations living there. This was God's command.

Moses said, "When the Lord your God brings you into the land you are entering to possess and drives out before you many nations,. . . . and when the Lord your God has delivered them over to you and you have defeated them, then you must destroy them totally. Make no treaty with them and show them no mercy. Do not intermarry with them. . . . for they will turn your children away from following me to serve other gods, and the Lord's anger will burn against you and will quickly destroy you. . . . Do not look on them with pity and do not serve their gods, for that will be a snare to you." Again Moses said, "Completely destroy them. . . . as the Lord your God has commanded you. Otherwise, they will teach you to follow all the detestable things they do in worshipping their gods, and you will sin against the Lord your God."[4]

Once this was done, the Israelites must destroy all the idols in the land. Moses said, "Break down their altars, smash their sacred stones, cut down their Asherah poles, burn their idols in the fire. For you are a people holy to the Lord your God. . . . The images of their gods you are to burn in the fire. Do not covet the silver and gold on them, and do not take it for yourselves, or you will be ensnared by it, for it is detestable to the Lord your God. Do not bring a detestable thing into your house or you, like it, will be set apart for destruction. Utterly abhor and detest it, for it is set apart for destruction."[5]

The Israelites must also destroy the places of worship that were all through the land: holy hills and sacred spots where the Canaanites sacrificed to their gods. Moses commanded, "Destroy completely all those places on the high mountains and on the hills and under every spreading tree where the nations you are dispossessing worship their gods . . . and wipe out their names from those places."[6] They were to erase those places of worship from the land, lest they be tempted to use them in worshipping the Lord.

The Israelites were to go to the one place which God would choose when they wished to sacrifice to the Lord their God. Moses warned the people, "You must not worship the Lord your God in their way. But you are to seek the place the Lord your God will choose from among all your tribes to put his Name there for his dwelling. To that place you must go. There bring your burnt offerings and sacrifices, your tithes and special gifts. . . . There, in the presence of the Lord your God, you and your families shall eat and shall rejoice in everything. . . . because the Lord your God has blessed you." Moses warned the people, "Be careful not to sacrifice your burnt offerings anywhere you please. Offer them only at the place the Lord will choose in one of your tribes, and there observe everything I command you."[7]

It was not just the Canaanites' places of worship that the Israelites must not use—God's people must also avoid imitating any of the other nations' worship practices or rituals. Moses warned the Israelites, "The Lord your God will cut off before you the nations you are about to invade and dispossess. But when you have driven them out and settled in their land, and after they have been destroyed before you, be careful not to be ensnared by inquiring about their gods, saying, 'How do these nations serve their gods? We will do the same.' You must not worship the Lord your God in their way, because in worshipping their gods, they do all kinds of detestable things the Lord hates."[8] Later, Moses warned the people against some of the specific things the Lord hated, telling them, "When you enter the land the Lord your God is giving you, do not learn to imitate the detestable ways of the nations there. Let no one be found among you who sacrifices his son or daughter in the fire, who practices divination or sorcery, interprets omens, engages in witchcraft, or casts spells, or who is a medium or spiritist or who consults the dead. Anyone who does these things is detestable to the Lord, and because of these detestable practices the Lord your God will drive out those nations before you. You must be blameless before the Lord your God."[9]

The Lord was very serious that the Israelites must avoid anything that would turn their hearts away from him. In fact, they must execute anyone who tried to turn them away from the Lord to worship other gods. Even if that person was a preacher or a prophet, a family member or a close friend, they must be put to death. Moses said, "If a prophet, or one who foretells by dreams, appears among you and announces to you a miraculous sign or wonder, and if the sign or wonder takes place, and he says, 'Let us follow other gods . . . and let us worship them,' you must not listen to the words of that prophet or dreamer. The Lord your God is testing you to find out whether you love him with all your heart and with all your soul. It is the Lord your God you must follow, and him you must revere. Keep his commands and obey him. Serve him and hold fast to him. That prophet or dreamer must be put to death, because he preached rebellion against the Lord your God. . . . He has tried to turn you from the way the Lord your God commanded you to follow. You must purge the evil from among you."

Moses said they must do this even if the evil person were "your very own brother, or your son or daughter, or the wife you love, or your closest friend."[10] Any time there was a report of someone who was "doing evil in the eyes of the Lord your God in violation of his covenant, and contrary to my command has worshipped other gods, bowing down to them or to the sun or the moon or the stars of the sky," then the matter must be investigated thoroughly. "If it is true and it has been proved that this detestable thing has been done in Israel," Moses commanded, "take the man or woman who has done this evil deed to your city gate and stone that person to death. . . . You must purge the evil from among you."[11]

And if a whole town in Israel was worshipping false idols and other gods, then (after a thorough investigation) the entire town was to be put to death. Moses said, "If it is true and it has been proved that this detestable thing has been done among you, you must certainly put to the sword all who live in that town. Destroy it completely . . . Burn the town and all its plunder as a whole burnt offering to the Lord your God. . . . It is to remain a ruin forever, never to be rebuilt."[12] Death was the penalty for disobeying the first and second commandments.

The Israelites were to worship God according to all his commands. They were to celebrate their sacred festivals to the Lord—the Feast of Unleavened Bread, the Feast of Weeks and the Feast of Tabernacles.[13] Observing these ceremonies was their religious duty. And true religion—serving and following the Lord—must be maintained in Israel.[14]

The Commandments About Loving People

The last six commandments deal with loving other people. When Jesus was asked to declare which commandment was the most important one, he told the people the two most important commandments. He told us that the most important one was to love God. And the second most important? "'Love your neighbour as yourself.' There is no commandment greater than these."[15] Jesus declared that "all the law and the prophets hang on these two commandments."[16] Another time Jesus taught what we call the Golden Rule: he said, "In everything, do to others what you would have them do to you, for this sums up the law and the prophets."[17]

God's law made it very clear that we are not to hurt or harm other people in any way (not even with our words or in our thoughts); rather, we are to help them whenever we can—even people we consider enemies.[18] The New Testament tells us, "He who loves his fellow man has fulfilled the law. The commandments . . . are summed up in this one rule: 'Love your neighbour as yourself.' Love does no harm to its neighbour. Therefore Love is the fulfilment of the law."[19]

5. Honour your father and mother.
6. You shall not murder.
7. You shall not commit adultery.
8. You shall not steal.
9. You shall not give false testimony against your neighbour.
10. You shall not covet. You shall not set your desire on . . . anything that belongs to your neighbour.

These laws were to govern the nation of Israel, regulating their relationships with one another and protecting everyone. If the Israelites applied and enforced these laws according to God's Word, then they would have a great nation known for its justice.[20]

What is justice? How can people know if the laws in their land are good and right and true? God graciously gave Israel a perfect standard of justice to govern their nation when he gave them the laws found in Deuteronomy. Every nation on earth could adopt these laws as their own, for now the Word of God and the laws of the Lord have gone forth to the ends of the earth. In fact, we can see that God's law is reflected in the laws of all nations, although not perfectly. The nations often do by nature the things required in God's law, because God's law is written on the hearts of all people.[21]

However, in some nations the penalties for breaking certain laws are too harsh, like punishing thieves by chopping off their hands (or sometimes even their heads). Such laws may be effective, stopping thieves from ever stealing again—but is this just? If we measure this law against God's perfect standard, we see that, although it upholds the eighth commandment in recognizing that stealing is wrong, nevertheless it falls far short of justice. In the law of the Lord a thief's hands were not to be chopped off. Rather, God required that the thief use his hands to pay back more than he had stolen.

In other nations the penalties for breaking certain laws are too lax and soft. In some countries (such as Canada) murderers are not executed anymore. These violent criminals are sometimes freed from prison only to repeat their vicious crimes. Is this really a good or right way of dealing with murderers? If we measure such lenient laws against God's perfect standard, we see that, although they uphold the sixth commandment by recognizing that murder is wrong, nevertheless they fall short of justice. In the law of the Lord murder was always considered a crime deserving death.

In Deuteronomy, Moses teaches Israel how to apply and enforce these commandments, so that righteousness, and not wickedness, would flourish in the Promised Land. Not only would Israel be a land flowing with milk and honey, it would also be a nation flowing with justice and righteousness.[22] Let us look more closely at the commandments dealing with people.

Honour your father and your mother.

Honour your father and your mother, as the lord your God has commanded you, so that you may live long and that it may go well with you in the land the lord your God is giving you.

Righteous, justice-seeking citizens would arise from God-fearing, parent-honouring children. The greatness of the nation would be found and formed in its homes, by its families. Deuteronomy does not speak much about the fifth commandment, but one can go to Proverbs to find many exhortations to obey this holy law: "Listen, my son, to your father's instruction and do not forsake your mother's teaching. A wise son brings joy to his father, but a foolish man despises his mother. To have a fool for a son brings grief; there is no joy for the father of a fool. If a man curses his father or mother, his lamp will be snuffed out in pitch darkness.[23] The eye that mocks a father, that scorns obedience to a mother, will be pecked out by the ravens of the valley, and be eaten by the vultures."[24] Death and darkness—that was the warning to all those men and women who disobeyed God's holy law and dishonoured the parents whom they should have loved.

It was the law in Israel for children to honour their parents—and this was a good and just law given by God for the preservation of their nation. But was there any way of enforcing this law? In Deuteronomy we find a terrifying statement about the fifth commandment: "If a man has a stubborn and rebellious son, who does not obey his father and mother and will not listen to them when they discipline him, his father and mother shall take hold of him and bring him to the elders at the gate of his town.[25] They shall say to the elders, 'This son of ours is stubborn and rebellious. He will not obey us. He is a profligate and a drunkard.'" They would bear witness before the judges that their son was a man who had entrenched himself in evil, destroying not only himself but also his whole family. If the elders weighed the evidence and found the man to be guilty, then a very severe penalty was imposed: "All the men of his town shall stone him to death."[26] Execution was the penalty for the complete renunciation of the fifth commandment. The severity of the punishment shows the gravity of the command. One can only imagine how evil a man must be for a father and mother to seek such a desperate remedy for one of their children.[27]

What Jesus taught about honouring parents.

Jesus rebuked the Jews who were not caring for their parents, reminding them that the command of God was this: "'Honour your father and mother,' and 'Anyone who curses his father or mother must be put to death.'"[28] Jesus taught this commandment not only by the words he spoke, but also by the life he lived. The Son of God was perfectly obedient to his Father in heaven. "He humbled himself and became obedient to death—even death on a cross."[29] Jesus was also obedient to his earthly parents. Even when Jesus was twelve years old—entering his teen years—we read that he was obedient to his parents—though he was the perfect Son of God and they were sinful human parents, often making mistakes in what they said and did.[30] Jesus' first miraculous sign was at his mother's request, and he took care of his mother even when he was dying on the cross, making sure that one of his disciples would look after her in her old age.[31]

What the New Testament says about honouring parents.

Romans speaks about people who are filled with every kind of wickedness, and we read in the long list of their evil practices that "they disobey their parents."[32] In other epistles, children are instructed to honour their parents for their own good, and to please their heavenly Father: "Children, obey your parents in the Lord, for this is right. 'Honour your father and mother,' which is the first commandment with a promise: 'that it may go well with you and that you may enjoy long life on the earth.' "Children, obey your parents in everything, for this pleases the Lord."[33]

You shall not murder.

Murder and assault were treated seriously and severely in Israel.[34] The punishment for murderers was execution—a man paid for a person's life by forfeiting his own. This was God's law expressly revealed to man from the earliest of days. The Lord said to Noah after the flood, "From each man . . . I will demand an accounting for the life of his fellow man. Whoever sheds the blood of man, by man shall his blood be shed; for in the image of God has God made man."[35] It was a law that went back to the very beginning, to the very creation of man in the image of God.

What would happen if someone killed another person by accident? When the Israelites settled in the Promised Land, they were to set up three cities of refuge in three sections of the country, with good roads built to them so that everyone had easy access to these cities.[36] Anyone who accidentally killed another person could flee to a city of refuge and have a safe place to stay. Moses said, "One who kills his neighbour unintentionally, without malice aforethought . . . may flee to one of these cities and save his life. Otherwise, the avenger of blood may pursue him in a rage, overtake him if the distance is too great, and kill him, even though he is not deserving of death, since he did it to his neighbour [accidentally] without malice aforethought. This is why I command you to set aside for yourselves three cities . . . so that innocent blood will not be shed in the land."[37]

What would happen to a man guilty of premeditated murder if he fled to a city of refuge to escape justice? In this situation Moses said, "If a man hates his neighbour and lies in wait for him, assaults and kills him, and then flees to one of these cities, the elders of his town shall send for him, bring him back from that city, and hand him over to the avenger of blood to die. Show him no pity. You must purge from Israel the guilt of shedding innocent blood, so that it may go well with you."[38]

God also commanded that people not be negligent in protecting other people from possibly harmful accidents. For example, Moses said, "When you build a new house, make a parapet around your roof so that you may not bring the guilt of bloodshed on your house if someone falls from the roof."[39] Another example was the law that demanded a vicious bull must be penned, so that no one would be gored by it accidentally. If a bull gored and killed someone because its owner did not take the trouble and expense to protect his neighbours, that man would be held accountable for murder.[40]

What Jesus taught about murder.

Jesus told the Jews, "You have heard that [Moses] said to the people long ago, 'Do not murder, and anyone who murders will be subject to judgement.' But I tell you that anyone who is angry with his brother will be subject to judgement."[41] Jesus taught that even secret anger and buried hatred in our hearts towards another person will not go unnoticed by God. He commanded instead, "Love your enemies, do good to those who hate you, bless those who curse you, pray for those who mistreat you. If someone strikes you on one cheek, turn to him the other also."[42] Jesus showed us this kind of love by his own example. He did good to everyone, even his enemies. He helped and healed, never hurting or harming. Even when he was dying on the cross, he prayed for his enemies, "Father, forgive them."[43] Jesus commanded us to love other people in this same way: "As I have loved you, so you must love one another."[44]

What the New Testament says about murder.

The New Testament teaches us that murderers will not be in heaven. "Their place will be in the fiery lake of burning sulphur."[45] We also read that "the wrath of God is being revealed from heaven against all the godlessness and wickedness of men"—men who are filled with every kind of evil, including murder and malice.[46] Even if we do not actually commit murder, "the acts of the sinful nature are obvious" and odious to God, who can see the secret sins of our hearts and lives: "hatred, discord, jealousy, fits of rage, selfish ambition, dissensions, factions, envy. . . . Those who live like this will not inherit the kingdom of God. But the fruit of the Spirit is love."[47] God commands that our hearts not be filled with hatred and rage, nor our thoughts with murder and malice. He has redeemed us from these wicked desires![48] There is to be something else in our hearts and in our lives—and that something is love.[49] "Get rid of all bitterness, rage, and anger . . . along with every form of malice. Be kind and compassionate to one another, forgiving each other, just as in Christ God forgave you. Be imitators of God, therefore, and live a life of love."[50]

You shall not commit adultery.

Unfaithfulness in marriage was a very serious matter to God. Adultery was a capital crime in Israel—punishable by execution. Like idolatry, it was the breaking of a sacred covenant; like murder, it was the killing of a marriage and a family. We live in a society where adultery is not viewed as a crime because it is so commonplace, but marriage was carefully protected in Israel.[51]

The penalty for adultery was severe according to God's law, but there was no double standard—God's commands applied equally to both men and women. This is unlike many cultures, both modern and ancient, where only the women are punished for sexual sins. God's law demanded that "both the adulterer and the adulteress must be put to death. If a man is found sleeping with another man's wife, both the man who slept with her and the woman must die."[52]

What Jesus said about adultery.

Jesus taught, "You have heard it said, 'Do not commit adultery.' But I tell you that anyone who looks at a woman lustfully has already committed adultery with her in his heart."[53] Once again, Jesus not only upheld this commandment, but extended it to the secret regions of the heart and the mind. It was not enough to be outwardly clean, keeping up an appearance of faithfulness and holiness, when inwardly a person was desiring in his heart to commit adultery and imagining in his mind the pleasures of that sin. Jesus condemned such hypocrisy, saying, "Woe to you . . . hypocrites! You are like whitewashed tombs, which look beautiful on the outside but on the inside are full of dead men's bones and everything unclean. In the same way, on the outside you appear to people as righteous but on the inside you are full of hypocrisy and wickedness."[54] Jesus was concerned that both a person's life and heart were pure.

Jesus also taught about marriage and divorce. Once, some experts in the law came to test and trap Jesus about this issue; they asked, "Is it lawful for a man to divorce his wife for any and every reason?" Jesus answered them according to God's law as it was instituted at creation. He said, "Haven't you read that in the beginning the Creator 'made them male and female,' and said, 'For this reason a man will leave his father and mother and be united to his wife, and the two will become one flesh?' So they are no longer two . . . but one. Therefore, what God has joined together, let man not separate."[55] But the experts in the law argued with Jesus. "Why then," they asked, "did Moses command that a man give his wife a certificate of divorce and send her away?" Jesus said, "Moses permitted you to divorce your wives because your hearts were hard, but it was not this way from the beginning."[56]

What God intended was for a man and a woman to be united together in love until death parted them. A man was to love, honour, and care for his wife.[57] But what would happen if a man married a woman and then hated her, refusing to obey God and love his wife? How unhappy such a woman must be! Moses permitted such hard-hearted men to divorce their wives, provided that they wrote them a certificate of divorce—that is, a binding legal document, that dissolved the marriage and allowed the woman the freedom to find love and joy with another man in another marriage.[58] The man could not just send his wife away in a moment of rage and then call her back whenever he felt like it, making her life miserable for as long as she lived. No, if the man refused to honour the vows of his marriage—if he was determined to get rid of his wife—then he was permitted to divorce her properly, with a finality that set her free.

In this sinful world, Moses permitted this evil to exist, but was God pleased with it? "I hate divorce," says the Lord God of Israel. The prophet Malachi warned that God would not hear the prayers of hard-hearted men who refused to love their wives, "You weep and wail because he no longer pays attention. . . . You ask 'Why?' It is because the Lord is acting as a witness between you and the wife of your youth, because you have broken faith with her, though she is your partner, the wife of your marriage covenant. . . . Guard yourself . . . and do not break faith with the wife of your youth."[59] And Jesus said, "I tell you that anyone who divorces his wife—except for marital unfaithfulness—and marries another woman, commits adultery."[60] These hard-hearted men thought that the law of God and the words of Moses allowed them to lust after other women and divorce their own wives at will, but Jesus told them plainly that God's law allowed them no loopholes for their sinful lusts and acts. They were breaking God's seventh commandment.

What the New Testament teaches about adultery.

In the New Testament we read, "Among you there must not be even a hint of sexual immorality or of any kind of impurity . . . because these are improper for God's holy people. For of this you can be sure: no immoral or impure person . . . has any inheritance in the kingdom of Christ and of

God. . . . Because of such things God's wrath comes on those who are disobedient. Be careful, then, how you live."[61] We must be careful that we live as redeemed children of God, rejecting the ways of those who do not know him, and learning to control our naturally sinful desires.[62] We are told, "Flee from sexual immorality. All other sins a person commits are outside his body, but the one who sins sexually sins against his own body. Do you not know that your body is the temple of the Holy Spirit, who is in you, whom you have received from God? You are not your own; you were bought at a price. Therefore, honour God with your body."[63]

You shall not steal.

God is concerned that we not participate in any kind of dishonest dealings. We must not steal or cheat one another, which is a kind of stealing. In fact, the law of love demands that we protect other people's property, giving instead of stealing, and helping instead of cheating. We have a saying: "Finders keepers, losers weepers." But that was not the law God gave his people. Moses said, "If you see your brother's ox or sheep straying, do not ignore it, but be sure to take it back to him. Do the same if you find your brother's donkey or his cloak or anything he loses. Do not ignore it."[64]

There were many specific ways God instructed the Israelites not to steal from one another. Sometimes people cheated by using smaller weights and measures when they were selling, and larger ones when they were buying. Moses said, "You must have accurate and honest weights and measures, so that you may live long in the land the Lord your God is giving you. For the Lord your God detests anyone . . . who deals dishonestly."[65] Another way people would steal was by secretly moving border lines, extending their own property and taking their neighbour's land. Moses commanded, "Do not move your neighbour's boundary stone."[66]

The people must not steal from God either by withholding the tithe. "Be sure to set aside a tenth of all that your fields produce each year," Moses instructed. This tithe was used to worship the Lord "at the place he will choose as a dwelling for his name, so that you may learn to revere the Lord always." There they would celebrate in the presence of the Lord, eating and drinking and rejoicing. This tithe was also given to the priests and shared with the poor, so that they too "could eat and be satisfied, and so that the Lord your God may bless you in all the work of your hands."[67]

Instead of stealing, Moses commanded the Israelites to be generous. "At the end of every seven years you must cancel debts. If there is a poor man among your brothers in any of the towns that the Lord your God is giving you, do not be hard-hearted or tightfisted toward your poor brother. Rather, be openhanded and freely lend him whatever he needs. . . . Give generously to him and do so without a grudging heart; then because of this the Lord your God will bless you in all your work and in everything you put your hand to. There will always be poor people in the land. Therefore I command you to be openhanded toward your brothers and toward the poor and needy in the land." [68]

What Jesus said about stealing.

Once again Jesus was concerned about the state of our hearts. We might not be thieves, but what is most important to us? What do our hearts desire and treasure? Jesus taught, "Do not store up for yourselves treasure on earth. . . . Store up for yourselves treasure in heaven. . . . For where your treasure is, there your heart will be also. No one can serve two masters. You cannot serve both God and money."[69]

Just obeying the command not to steal was not enough. Jesus also taught we must give instead of stealing from one another. He said, "Give and it will be given to you. A good measure, pressed down, shaken together, and running over, will be poured into your lap. For with the measure you use, it will be measured to you."[70]

One time a man came up to Jesus and asked what he must do to inherit eternal life. "Jesus answered, 'You know the commandments: Do not murder, do not commit adultery, do not steal, do not give false testimony, do not defraud, honour your father and mother.' 'Teacher,' he declared, 'all these I have kept since I was a boy.' Jesus looked at him and loved him. 'One thing you lack,' he said. 'Go, sell everything you have and give to the poor, and you will have treasure in heaven. Then come, follow me.'"[71]

What the New Testament teaches about stealing.

"Neither . . . thieves, nor the greedy, . . . nor swindlers will inherit the kingdom of God."[72] Stealing is not a practice that can be part of the Christian life. The New Testament instructs those whose sinful natures incline towards this kind of dishonesty that, "he who has been stealing must steal no longer, but must work, doing something useful with his own hands, that he may have something to share with those in need."[73] In fact, all of God's people are called to be generous—it is not enough merely to avoid stealing or cheating; we must give. "Remember this: Whoever sows sparingly will also reap sparingly, and whoever sows generously will also reap generously. Each man should give what he has decided in his heart to give, not reluctantly or under compulsion, for God loves a cheerful giver. And God is able to make all grace abound to you, so that in all things and at all times, having all that you need, you will abound in every good work. You will be made rich in every way so that you can be generous on every occasion, and . . . your generosity will result in thanksgiving to God."[74]

You shall not give false testimony against your neighbour.

"Do not lie. Do not deceive one another. Do not pervert justice . . . but judge your neighbour fairly. Do not go about spreading slander among your people."[75] Spreading lies about someone is called slander, and it is considered a crime. Telling lies in a court of law is called perjury, and this is a very serious crime, for a witness has taken an oath (on the Bible) to tell the truth, the whole truth and nothing but the truth.

In the book of Proverbs, the ninth commandment is expressed many times in many ways. Dishonesty is described as something the Lord hates, and as something that is harmful to all involved—including the false witness himself.[76] "Do not testify against your neighbour without cause or use your lips to deceive. Whoever spreads slander is a fool. . . . With his mouth the godless destroys his neighbour. He who guards his mouth and his tongue keeps himself from calamity. A false witness will perish, and whoever listens to him will be destroyed forever."[77]

If a witness was caught lying, the penalty was severe. Moses said, "One witness is not enough to convict a man accused of any crime or offense he may have committed. A matter must be established by the testimony of two or three witnesses. . . . The judges must make a thorough investigation, and if the witness proves to be a liar, giving false testimony against his brother, then do to him as he intended to do to his brother. You must purge the evil from among you. The rest of the people will hear of this and be afraid, and never again will such an evil thing be done among you. Show no pity: life for life, eye for eye, tooth for tooth, hand for hand, foot for foot."[78]

What Jesus said about false testimony.

In speaking about the devil, the deceiver who leads the whole world astray, Jesus said, "There is no truth in him. When he lies, he speaks his native language, for he is a liar and the father of lies."[79] But Jesus always spoke the truth.[80] "No deceit was found in his mouth;" no lie ever left his lips. He not only spoke truth, he was truth.[81] Jesus Christ is "the faithful witness," the one "who is holy and true," whose name is "Faithful and True."[82]

What the New Testament teaches about false testimony.

No one "who loves and practices falsehood" will see the kingdom of God.[83] "All liars—their place will be in the fiery lake of burning sulphur. This is the second death."[84] As Christians and as servants of God, we must commend ourselves to people by truthful and simple speech. "We have renounced secret and shameful ways; we do not use deception, nor do we distort the Word of God. On the contrary, by setting forth the truth plainly we commend ourselves to every man's conscience in the sight of God." We are exhorted to speak the truth in love, because deception does not belong to our new nature. "You were taught, with regard to your former way of life, to put off your old self, which is being corrupted by its deceitful desires; to be made new in the attitude of your minds; and to put on the new self, created to be like God in true righteousness and holiness. Therefore, each of you must put off falsehood and speak truthfully to his neighbour."[85]

You shall not covet.

You shall not covet. You shall not set your desire
on anything that belongs to your neighbour.

The tenth commandment deals with the dark regions of the heart, where our secret desires lie hidden. But God sees all the deepest desires of our hearts, whether they are good or bad.[86] A covetous person is a person greedy for gain; his eyes and heart are set on getting what he wants no matter what he has to do, even if that means using immoral or illegal ways to gain it. Woe to the man who is motivated by greed and whose heart is filled with every kind of covetous desire. "Woe to him who builds his house by unjust gain." Woe to the man whose life's longings and dearest dreams are accomplished by "an evil covetousness."[87]

What Jesus said about covetousness.

Jesus taught that the evil desires of a man's heart are what make him unclean. "For from within, out of men's hearts, come evil thoughts," and those thoughts produce all kinds of wickedness.[88] He warned us, "Watch out! Be on your guard against all kinds of greed! A man's life does not consist in the abundance of his possessions. Take heed and beware of covetousness."[89] Jesus also said, "What shall it profit a man, if he shall gain the whole world, and lose his own soul?"[90] We must be careful how we live. It is so easy to fall into the trap of living for ourselves, storing up treasures on earth, and seeking to make ourselves rich, instead of storing up treasures in heaven and seeking to make ourselves rich towards God.

What the New Testament teaches about covetousness

God's Word in the New Testament teaches that covetousness or greediness is a kind of idolatry—which is a very serious sin indeed. "For of this you can be sure: No . . . greedy [or covetous] person—such a man is an idolater—has any inheritance in the kingdom of Christ and of God. . . . Because of such things God's wrath comes on those who are disobedient."[91] We must not be greedy covetous people always craving financial gain. "But godliness with contentment is great gain. For we brought nothing into the world, and we can take nothing out of it. But if we have food and clothing, we will be content with that. People who want to get rich fall into temptation and a trap and into many foolish and harmful desires that plunge men into ruin and destruction. For the love of money is the root of all kinds of evil. Some people, eager for money, have wandered from the faith and pierced themselves with many griefs. . . . Flee from all this and [instead of chasing after money] pursue righteousness, godliness, faith, love."[92]

Contentment is the opposite of covetousness. We are commanded in the New Testament, "Keep your lives free from the love of money and be content with what you have, because God has said, 'Never will I leave you; never will I forsake you.' So we say with confidence, 'The Lord is my helper; I will not be afraid.'"[93] We can rest secure, we can be content, we can live in peace—for God is with us.

Our hope and our trust must be in God, not in our wealth. If we live this way, trusting in God, we will be content whatever happens to us. We will echo in our hearts the words of the apostle Paul: "I have learned to be content whatever the circumstances. I know what it is to be in need, and I know what it is to have plenty. I have learned the secret of being content in any and every situation. . . . I can do everything through him who gives me strength."[94]

> Blessed is the man whose delight is in the law of the Lord. Blessed is the man who makes the Lord his trust. Blessed is the man who fears the Lord, who finds great delight in his commands. Blessed are they whose ways are blameless, who walk according to the law of the Lord. Blessed are they who keep his statutes and seek him with all their heart. Blessed are all those who fear the Lord, who walk in his ways. Blessed are all who take refuge in him.[95]

LESSON 5: TEACHER'S GUIDE

The Ten Commandments . . . Again

Deuteronomy means "second law" and we would be remiss in not dealing thoroughly with God's law this second time, which is obviously what God intended for all of us—a thorough review of all the commandments. I suggest dividing this lesson into seven sections: the commandments about loving God could be the first session and then perhaps one session for each of the last six commandments.

VISUAL AIDS:

The Ten Commandments should elicit much discussion. You and your students can collect newspaper or magazine clippings about the breaking and the keeping of each of the commandments, including the ones about loving God, which are certainly relevant to our modern culture.

MEMORY WORK:

I am assuming that the children already know the Ten Commandments from previous study, although you may want to review with them. Here are other Scriptures to memorize. I've put them in Q&A format to highlight for the children the emphasis of each verse.

1. Q. Which is the greatest commandment in the law?

   A. Jesus answered, "Love the Lord your God with all your heart and with all your soul and with all your mind. This is the first and greatest commandment. And the second is like it: Love your neighbour as yourself. All the law and the prophets hang on these two commandments." Matthew 22:37–40[96]

2. Q. What is the Golden Rule?

   A. Jesus said: "Love your enemies, do good to those who hate you, bless those who curse you, pray for those who mistreat you. . . . Do to others as you would have them do to you." Luke 6:31

3. Q. What is the Royal Law?

   A. "If you really keep the royal law found in Scripture—Love your neighbour as yourself—you are doing right." James 2:8

4. Q. What is the fulfilment of the law?

   A. "He who loves his fellow man has fulfilled the law. The commandments . . . are summed up in this one rule: Love your neighbour as yourself. Love does no harm to its neighbour. Therefore Love is the fulfilment of the law." Romans 13:8–10

5. Q. What was Jesus' new commandment?

   A. Jesus said, "A new command I give you: Love one another. As I have loved you, so you must love one another." John 13:4

   Again Jesus said, "My command is this: Love one another as I have loved you." John 15:12

   A third time Jesus said, "This is my command: Love one another." John 15:17

6. Q. How can a person be blessed?

   A. "Blessed is the man . . . whose delight is in the Law of the Lord." Psalm 1:1–2

   "Blessed is the man who makes the Lord his trust." Psalm 40:4

   "Blessed is the man who fears the Lord, who finds great delight in his commands." Psalm 112:1

   "Blessed are all who take refuge in him." Psalm 2:12

REVIEW QUESTIONS:

1. When did God first give the Ten Commandments to Israel? Whose voice did the people hear?
2. When did God give the Ten Commandments to Israel a second time? Whose voice did the people hear then?
3. How blessed these people were to hear the voice of God and the voice of Moses declaring to them the Ten Commandments! Was there another generation of Jews so blessed? Whose voice did they hear declaring the law of God?

4. Jesus, the Son of God, said he had not come to abolish God's law. What did he come to do?
5. The Israelites were about to enter and possess a good land, flowing with milk and honey, but also filled with evil. How was it polluted with wickedness?
6. What must the Israelites do to clean away the filth of wickedness? What must they do to make it a holy land, instead of a filthy and defiled land?
7. What was the penalty for idolatry in Israel? Why did God—who is a God of Love—demand such a severe penalty for this crime?
8. What other crimes in Israel were considered deserving of the death penalty? What was the punishment for a thief?
9. Jesus was concerned not only that our lives would be free from crime, but that our hearts would be free from sin. The sixth commandment says, "Do not commit murder." What did Jesus teach? The seventh commandment says, "Do not commit adultery." What did Jesus teach?
10. Jesus said, "Watch out! Be on your guard against all kinds of greed! Beware of covetousness." Why is this such a deadly sin? Instead of being greedy and covetous, what must we be?

PRAYERS:

1. O God, how great is your Love for us! Help us to love you. May your Holy Spirit work mightily in us to love you with all our heart, all our soul, all our mind, and all our strength. O Lord, let us hold back nothing of ourselves from you, for you held nothing back in your Love for us. You gave us your one and only son, Jesus Christ, to die as a sacrifice for our sins. Lord, thank you for such a great Love! Help us also to love one another. Amen.
2. Our heavenly Father, thank you for giving us earthly fathers and mothers to care for us. Help us to love our parents and listen to them. Help us to obey them, even when we don't want to. O Lord, give us hearts that desire to do what is right. Deliver us from evil. Amen.

3. O Lord our God, who has made and loved us all, help us to be like you. Help us to love all people and do good to everyone. We thank you for your holy Word, for your perfect law. Lord Jesus, help us to obey your new commandment to love one another. Amen.
4. Lord, we thank you for making human beings male and female. We thank you for creating marriage and blessing the union between a man and a woman. We thank you for our families, for bringing children into the world, for giving us brothers and sisters, for blessing us with babies. How good you are, O Lord! How wonderful are your works! How bountiful is your Love and your grace! Please, Lord, protect and unite our families in unbreakable bonds of love. Keep our families safe from all the wicked assaults of the evil one, who desires to divide, deceive, and destroy. Whom God has joined together, let no one—not even the devil himself—tear asunder. O Lord, we look to you for help and strength. Amen.
5. O Lord our God, who has freely given us every good thing, we thank you. Give us grateful hearts and giving hands. O Lord, keep us from greedy hearts and grasping hands. Forgive our sins, O God. Amen.
6. O Lord our God, we thank you that you have not hidden your Word from us, but you have told us the truth. Help us to always speak truth. Keep us from telling lies, spreading lies, or believing lies. Deliver us from the evil one, who was a liar from the beginning. Help us to daily follow Jesus, the faithful and true witness. O Lord, help us to put our hope and our trust and our faith in the One who loved us and gave himself for us. Amen.
7. O Lord, create in us a new heart—a heart filled with praise and thanks to you. Help us to learn the secret of being content in any and every situation. Help us to trust in you. Amen.

PSALMS TO SING:

The psalms are filled with praise for God's law and God's Word, with exhortations for us to study and obey all his commandments.

1A; 19B; 37E; 40CE; 78A; 112AB; 119

Lesson 6

PROPHECIES OF VICTORY

• Deuteronomy 7

The Israelites were on the edge of the Promised Land and the verge of war. Moses would be gone before the great conquest of Canaan began, so he would not lead his soldiers into battle, but he would leave them with a weapon sharper than any double-edged sword—the Word of God. Moses, the prophet of the Lord, left the Israelites with God's promises of victory. Imagine how boldly they could march and how fiercely they could fight, knowing beforehand that they would win the war!

Moses spoke many times to the Israelites about their conquest of the Promised Land, showing his complete faith in God's Word by saying "when," not "if." He always said, "When the Lord your God has destroyed the nations whose land he is giving you and when you have driven them out and settled in their towns and houses"[1]—then they must begin to build up the holy land according to the Lord's commands. Moses never suggested that God might not actually give them the Promised Land. Victory was not just a possibility, it was a certainty on which they could base all their other plans.

However sure God's promises of victory, the Israelites were also certain that their enemies were larger and stronger than they were. If God's people assessed the situation by sight rather than by faith—if they simply looked at the enormous armies and towering cities facing them—then they had every reason to be terrified.

Moses was well aware of the strength of their enemies. He knew they must attack nations that had fortified cities surrounded by walls that were impossible to scale because they were so high, and impossible to smash because they were so wide. These cities were the strongholds of Satan—and the demons themselves would fight to defend their fortresses of wickedness!

Moses knew that these nations had terrifying armies with fierce soldiers that were as strong and as tall as giants. Who could fight hand-to-hand against such monsters and survive? But Moses promised his men victory against them, urging the people to look to the Lord, remembering what he had already done for them and looking forward to what he would still do. Moses said, "Do not be afraid of them! Remember well what the Lord your God did to Pharaoh and to all Egypt."[2]

The Israelites did not have to worry about people who were bigger and stronger than they were, because God was on their side and he was bigger and stronger than any of their enemies. Moses said, "Hear, O Israel. You are now about to cross the Jordan to go in and dispossess nations greater and stronger than you. . . . But be assured today that the Lord your God is the one who goes across ahead of you like a devouring fire. He will destroy them! He will subdue them before you and you will drive them out and annihilate them quickly, as the Lord has promised you."[3]

As they entered into war, the Israelites must not trust in themselves or their own strength. They must rely on God, believing in his strength and his Love for them.[4] It was because of God's Love—not because of anything in themselves or anything they had earned—that the Israelites were being given the Promised Land. Moses said, "Because he loved your forefathers and chose their descendants after them, he brought you out of Egypt by his presence and his great strength, to drive out before you nations greater and stronger than you and to bring you into their land to give it to you for an inheritance."[5] This war was based on the Love of God.

Again and again in Deuteronomy Moses assured the people of God's Love. It was not because they were a great people or even a good people that God loved them. No, it was because of the greatness and goodness of God. The Israelites had no reason to boast in themselves or trust in themselves. Let them boast in the Lord and trust in his Love. The Almighty King of heaven and earth was the one who chose them, saved them, and loved them! Moses said, "To the Lord your God belong the heavens, even the highest heavens, the earth, and everything in it. Yet the Lord set his affection on your forefathers and loved them, and he chose you, their descendants, above all the nations."[6]

As the Israelites faced the great war ahead of them, they could confidently say, "We are more than conquerors, because God loves us!"[7] Moses wanted the Israelites to march forth to war fortified with that great truth. If God was with them and for them, who could possibly prevail against them?

Moses wanted Israel's army to be continually encouraged with such prophecies of victory, so he appointed the priests who followed him to bless the soldiers. Moses told them, "When you are about to go into battle, the priest shall come forward and address the army, saying: 'Hear, O Israel, today you are going into battle against your enemies. Do not be fainthearted or afraid. Do not be terrified or give way to panic before them. For the Lord your God is the One who goes with you to fight for you against your enemies—to give you victory!'"[8]

As the time for him to die drew ever closer, Moses spoke to the whole congregation of Israel. He said, "I am now a hundred and twenty years old and I am no longer able to lead you. The Lord has said to me, 'You shall not cross the Jordan River.' The Lord your God himself will cross over ahead of you. He will destroy these nations before you and you will take possession of their land. . . . The Lord will deliver them to you, and you must do to them all that I have commanded you. Be strong and courageous. Do not be afraid or terrified because of them, for the Lord your God goes with you. He will never leave you nor forsake you."[9] These promises and prophecies of victory would give strength and courage to God's people as they entered into battle. Moses left the Israelites with a very great hope—the hope that they would surely win the war.

When the prophet who was greater than Moses appeared, he would give his soldiers similar words of encouragement. Jesus said to his followers, "Do not be afraid, little flock, for your Father has been pleased to give you the kingdom."[10] The kingdoms of this wicked world "will make war against the Lamb, but the Lamb will overcome them because he is the Lord of lords and King of kings—and with him will be his called, chosen, and faithful followers."[11] We also, like the Israelites, do not rely on our own strength but on the strength of him who chose and loves us. He is the one who has overcome the world.[12] "Thanks be to God! He gives us the victory through our Lord Jesus Christ." [13]

Moses encouraged the Israelites not to be afraid, "for the Lord your God goes with you he will never leave you nor forsake you."[14] But Jesus said, "Surely I am with you always, to the very end of the age."[15] If we trust in Jesus, we can go through this life unafraid because we know that he loves us and is with us. Along with the Israelites and Jesus' disciples, we can also be assured of God's Love.[16] We need not fear anyone or anything.

> Who shall separate us from the love of Christ? Shall trouble or hardship or persecution or famine or nakedness or danger or sword? No! In all these things we are more than conquerors through him who loved us. For I am convinced that neither death nor life, neither angels nor demons, neither the present nor the future, nor any powers, neither height nor depth, nor anything else in all creation, will be able to separate us from the Love of God that is in Christ Jesus our Lord![17]

LESSON 6: TEACHER'S GUIDE

Prophecies of Victory

VISUAL AIDS:

Show your students some photos of World War 2 soldiers joyfully giving the "V" sign with their fingers—"V for Victory!" When they entered the war, these modern soldiers had no promise from God of victory, but still they showed great courage.

You could also show your students pictures of people hugging (such as a parent hugging a child) or kissing (such as a groom kissing his bride). These are the ways we express our love.

MEMORY WORK:

"This is the victory that has overcome the world, even our faith! Who is it that overcomes the world? Only he who believes that Jesus is the Son of God."

1 John 5:4–5

"I am convinced that neither death nor life, neither angels nor demons, neither the present nor the future, nor any powers, neither height nor depth, nor anything else in all creation, will be able to separate us from the Love of God that is in Christ Jesus our Lord."

Romans 8:38–39

REVIEW QUESTIONS:

1. Before they went to war, Moses gave his soldiers a weapon that was sharper than any double-edged sword. What was it?
2. What did God promise the Israelite army again and again that would greatly encourage them in the war they must fight?

3. Describe the enemy cities and the enemy soldiers. What did Moses say to give the army of God courage to fight an enemy that was bigger and stronger than they were?
4. Why did God love the Israelites?
5. How long did Jesus say that he would be with us? How does that make you feel?
6. How did God show his Love for us?
7. What can separate us from the Love of God in Christ Jesus?

PRAYER:

Our heavenly Father, we thank you for your great Love for us, a Love which we do not deserve. O Lord, help us to trust daily in that Love, that we might march forward in our lives without fear. Help us to overcome the evil one. We thank you that we are more than conquerors through Christ who loved us and gave himself for us. We thank you also for your many great promises to us, especially the words of Jesus that he is with us always.

PSALMS TO SING:

These are songs of God's victory and our triumph in him:

"Clap your hands, all ye people! Shout to God with a voice of triumph! Hosanna! Hosanna!" (Psalm 47).

"O Lord . . . you will comfort me with songs of victory" (Psalm 32).

98A . . . and 18J; 32C; 45A; 47A; 59B (7, 12, 13); 64A (1, 9); 92A

There are many psalms that proclaim God's unfailing Love:

"O Lord . . . let Thy steadfast love cheer me" (Psalm 119).

57B (5, 9, 10); 86B . . . 13A (5); 25AB; 31C (11); 52B (3); 69C (11, 12); 89A (1); 103A; 106A; 108A; 109B; 115C (1, 4); 117AB; 118A; 119J (3); 136A (1, 2); 145B

Lesson 7

THE PROMISE OF THE PROPHET

• Deuteronomy 18:14–22

Long ago in the Garden of Eden, when sin and death entered the world, God gave the first man and woman hope in a great promise. He promised the human race a Saviour—one of the woman's offspring—who would crush that "serpent of old" called Satan, the tempter.[1] This was God's great promise from the beginning: that a Messiah would be born into the world to deliver God's people from Satan's power, freeing them from the grip of sin and death and hell.

When the Israelites arrived at the border of the Promised Land, it had been hundreds of years since God had last spoken of this Messiah to their forefathers long ago. God had said to Abraham, "All peoples on earth will be blessed through you;"[2] so they knew the Messiah would be a son of Abraham. God repeated the great promise to Abraham's son Isaac: "Through your offspring all nations on earth will be blessed,"[3] so they knew the Messiah would be a son of Isaac. Later God spoke in a dream to one of Isaac's twin sons, Jacob, again saying, "All peoples on earth will be blessed through you and your offspring";[4] so they knew that the Messiah would be a son of Jacob also.

Then Jacob had twelve sons. Through which son would God's great promise continue? As Jacob lay on his deathbed he prophesied, "The sceptre will not depart from Judah, nor the ruler's staff from between his feet, until he comes to whom it belongs and the obedience of the nations is his."[5] Thus they knew that the Messiah would be a son of Judah and he would be a great king to whom all nations ultimately would bow.

But now the Israelites were camped beside the Jordan River and hundreds of years had passed with no Messiah appearing. In fact, God had been strangely silent concerning this great promise. But now Moses, who spoke from God, told the Israelites a new piece of information about the Messiah: not only would he be a king; he also would be a truly great prophet—greater even than Moses, who would soon die. He left the people with this great hope: "The Lord your God will raise up for you a prophet like me from among your own brothers. you must listen to him."[6]

Forty years earlier when the Israelites had been camped at Mount Horeb, they had been terrified by the voice of the Lord speaking to them from the mountain, which was blazing with fire and swirling with darkness. At that time the people pleaded, "Let us not hear the voice of the Lord our God nor see this great fire anymore, or we will die." Then the Lord said to Moses, "What they say is good. I will raise up for them a prophet like you from among their brothers; I will put my words in his mouth, and he will tell them everything I command him. If anyone does not listen to my words that the prophet speaks in my name, I myself will call him to account."[7] Although God raised up many good and true prophets for Israel, we know that this passage referred particularly to the promised Messiah, who would be the greatest prophet of all.

In the New Testament, hundreds of years later, the Jews were still waiting for this prophet. When John the Baptist appeared, "the people were waiting expectantly and were all wondering in their hearts if John might possibly be the messiah."[8] But after Jesus' baptism in the Jordan River, John exclaimed, "I have seen and I testify that this is the Son of God!"[9]

Many people believed the testimony of John the Baptist and put their faith in Jesus. Other people believed in Jesus because of his own teaching—on hearing his words they said, "Surely this man is the prophet!"[10] One of the first disciples told his friend about Jesus declaring, "We have found the one Moses wrote about in the law, and about whom the prophets also wrote!"[11] Still others believed in Jesus because of his miracles. "After the people saw the miraculous sign that Jesus did [the feeding of five thousand people] they began to say, 'Surely this is the prophet who is to come into the world.'"[12]

The rest of the New Testament also confirms that Jesus was the prophet whom Moses had promised. When Peter was preaching the gospel to the Jews in Jerusalem, he quoted from Deuteronomy, proclaiming God's promise of the prophet and revealing to them that the prophet was Jesus Christ. Peter reminded them, "Moses said, 'The Lord your God will raise up for you a prophet like me from among your own people; you must listen to everything he tells you.'"[13] And Jesus himself said, "Moses wrote about me!"[14]

Fulfilling the Promise

The LORD your God will raise up for you a prophet like me from among your own brothers. You must listen to him. For this is what you asked of the LORD your God at Horeb on the day of the assembly when you said, "Let us not hear the voice of the LORD our God nor see this great fire anymore, or we will die." The LORD said to me, . . .I will raise up for them a prophet like you from among their brothers; I will put my words in his mouth, and he will tell them everything I command him. If anyone does not listen to my words that the prophet speaks in my name, I myself will call him to account."[15]

Jesus spoke the words of God.

Because the people could not bear to hear the terrifying voice of the Lord, God sent prophets—mere men like themselves—to speak for him. God raised up many prophets who spoke his word. However, Jesus was the prophet, who not only spoke the Word of God, he was the Word of God.[16] "In the past God spoke to our forefathers through the prophets at many times and in various ways, but in these last days he has spoken to us by his Son. The Son is the radiance of God's glory and the exact representation of his being, sustaining all things by his powerful Word."[17] God's voice from heaven testified concerning Jesus, "This is my Son, whom I love. Listen to him."[18]

John the Baptist also testified concerning Jesus, "The one whom God has sent speaks the words of God, for God gives [him] the Spirit without limit. The Father loves the Son and has placed everything in his hands. Whoever believes in the Son has eternal life, but whoever rejects the Son will not see life, for God's wrath remains on him."[19] It was just as God declared through Moses: "If anyone does not listen to my words that the prophet speaks in my name, I myself will call him to account." Accepting the command to listen to Jesus leads to eternal life and salvation, but rejecting that command leads to eternal death and damnation.

Jesus himself testified that the words he spoke came from the Father. Jesus cried out, "When a man believes in me, he does not believe in me only, but in the One who sent me. When he looks at me, he sees the One who sent me. For I did not speak of my own accord, but the Father who sent me commanded me what to say and how to say it. I know that his command leads to eternal life. So whatever I say is just what the Father told me to say."[20] Again Jesus said, "These words you hear are not my own; they belong to the Father who sent me."[21]

Jesus also testified that he was the promised prophet, sent into the world by God and anointed by the Holy Spirit, to proclaim the gospel to them. Surely these words of prophecy were the words of the prophet, Jesus: "Here I am; I have come. It is written about me in the scroll. I desire to do your will, O my God. Your law is within my heart. I proclaim righteousness in the great assembly. . . . I speak of your faithfulness and salvation. I do not conceal your Love and your truth from the great assembly."[22]

Jesus was unlike any other prophet in Israel in that he spoke the Word of God from within himself, for, as he testified, "I and the Father are one."[23] All Jesus' thoughts were God's thoughts; all Jesus' words were God's words—for he was God. How different this was from all the other prophets, who were sinners like the rest of us in thought, word, and deed.[24] Every other prophet in Israel, even Moses, brought the Word of God to the people, saying to them, "This is what God says," or "Thus says the Lord"[25]—but the prophet Jesus said, "Truly, truly, I say unto you."

Jesus was a prophet like Moses.

Over the years, God raised up many prophets in Israel, but there was no one like Moses. We read that after Moses' death, "no prophet has arisen in Israel like Moses, whom the Lord knew face to face, who did all those miraculous signs and wonders the Lord sent him to do in Egypt. . . . For no one has ever shown the mighty power or performed the awesome deeds that Moses did in the sight of all Israel."[26] The miracles that Moses performed validated his words and testified to the fact that he was a true prophet sent from God. Moses would be Israel's greatest prophet until the long-promised Messiah arrived.

Jesus also performed many miracles, and these attested to the fact that he was not only a prophet of God, but that he was the prophet promised by Moses. When John the Baptist sent his followers to ask Jesus if he was the One they were expecting, Jesus pointed to his miracles. He answered, "Go back and report to John what you hear and see: the blind receive sight, the lame walk, those who have leprosy are cured, the deaf hear, the dead are raised, and the good news is preached to the poor. Blessed is the man who does not fall away on account of me."[27] Many people in Israel believed in Jesus because of all the miraculous signs and wonders that he performed.[28] When other people asked Jesus, "How long will you keep us in suspense? If you are the Messiah, tell us plainly," Jesus answered, "I did tell you, but you do not believe. The miracles I do in my Father's name speak for me. . . . Even though you do not believe me, believe the miracles, that you may know and understand that the Father is in me, and I in the Father."[29]

Not only was Jesus like Moses, he was the only prophet in Israel who surpassed Moses. Moses delivered his people from an earthly evil empire and from the power of a mighty human ruler, but Jesus delivered all God's people forever, securing for them an eternal salvation from the powers of the evil one. "Jesus has been found worthy of greater honour than Moses!"[30]

Jesus was an Israelite man.

Although Jesus was the Son of God, he was "found in appearance as a man. He took the form of a servant, being made in human likeness."[31] He was God, but when he spoke the Israelites heard the voice of a man like themselves, which did not fill them with fear and dread. No one thought they would die just from listening to the voice of Jesus.

"Since the children have flesh and blood, he too shared in their humanity. He had to be made like his brothers in every way."[32] Jesus was born to an Israelite father and mother. The Jews never questioned that Jesus was a fellow Israelite, one of their own brothers. In this respect also, Jesus fulfilled the prophesy concerning the prophet whom God would raise up "from among your own brothers."

Jesus was a true prophet.

In Deuteronomy, Moses warned the people not to listen to the false prophets in the nations they were going to dispossess, because they practised sorcery and divination. The Israelites must listen only to the prophets whom God sent, looking to them alone for guidance and wisdom.

But how could the people distinguish between false prophets and true prophets, since both claimed to speak from the Lord their God? They must have some way to know when a message had not been spoken by the Lord. God told them, "If what a prophet proclaims in the name of the Lord does not take place or come true, that is a message the Lord has not spoken."[33]

Many false prophets and phony messiahs arose in Israel. Did Jesus pass the test of a true prophet? Did what he predict come to pass? When the Jews demanded a miraculous sign from him to prove his authority and authenticity as a prophet of the Lord, Jesus answered, "Destroy this temple and I will raise it again in three days."[34] Jesus was speaking of the temple of his own body, referring to his crucifixion and resurrection. The sign he gave the people was that he would be raised to life in three days! Again and again Jesus referred to this as the great sign that would prove he was the prophet promised by God.[35] Jesus did rise on the third day, proving he was not only a true prophet but the prophet—and the Son of God.[36]

One of the greatest gifts that Moses gave the Israelites in Deuteronomy was the promise of the prophet, giving them hope in the Messiah who was surely coming. And Jesus Christ was God's greatest gift, not only to Israel, but to the whole world!

LESSON 7: TEACHER'S GUIDE

The Promise of the Prophet

VISUAL AIDS:

A Bible that has Jesus' words in red letters would be an excellent thing to have for this lesson. Show your children that the red-lettered words are the words of the prophet promised by Moses in Deuteronomy.

MEMORY WORK:

> God's voice from heaven declared who Jesus was: "This is my beloved Son, whom I love. Listen to him."
>
> Mark 9:7

> "Whoever believes in the Son has eternal life, but whoever rejects the Son will not see life, for God's wrath remains on him."
>
> John 3:36

REVIEW QUESTIONS:

1. When did God first promise a Saviour who would crush Satan? At that time, who did God say it would be?
2. God said that the Messiah would be the Son of Abraham, Isaac, and Jacob. Which one of Jacob's twelve sons would be the forefather of the Messiah?
3. Jacob prophesied that the Messiah would be a king. What did Moses prophesy that the Messiah would be?
4. When John the Baptist appeared, people asked him if he was the Messiah, the promised prophet. What was his answer?
5. What did John say about Jesus?
6. Why was Jesus the greatest prophet—greater even than Moses?

7. Jesus performed many miracles to prove that he was a prophet sent from God. What kinds of things did he do?
8. What great event did Jesus foretell that came to pass, proving he was not only a prophet of God, but the very Son of God?

PRAYER:

Dear God, we thank you for the promise you gave Moses to encourage all the people: that you would send another prophet to them—and we thank you that you kept your Word and fulfilled your promise by sending us your son, Jesus Christ, the greatest prophet of all! We thank you, O God, for your faithfulness. you sent us a Saviour to rescue us from sin and death and all the power of the evil one. O Lord, help us to listen to him and to believe in him with all our hearts. Amen.

PSALMS TO SING:

God commanded his people to listen to the prophet whom he would send to speak his words and be his voice to the people. Here are psalms about the voice of God:

29A . . . and 50A; 68E; 77C; 85B

Lesson 8

RENEWAL OF THE COVENANT

• Deuteronomy 29

Moses would die soon, and there was still something very important that God had commanded Moses to do with the people. So Moses summoned all the Israelites to come before the Lord. Every single person was called to this assembly to stand in the presence of God. No one was too high or mighty to skip this meeting, nor was anyone too poor or lowly to not be invited; even the Israelites' servants and slaves—the foreigners who chopped their wood and hauled their water—must be present at this meeting. An elderly woman who could barely hobble to the meeting leaning on her cane—yes, she must be there. And a little newborn baby, swaddled and snuggled and sleeping in his mother's arms—yes, even he must come to meet with the Lord. What was happening this day that was so important?

Moses said, "All of you are standing today in the presence of the Lord your God. . . . You are standing here in order to enter into a covenant with the Lord your God, a covenant the Lord is making with you this day and sealing with an oath, to confirm you this day as his people, that he may be your God, just as he promised you and as he swore to your forefathers: Abraham, Isaac, and Jacob."[1] Moses was the mediator of this covenant, standing between God and the people—even those people in Israel who were not yet born, for the Lord is a faithful God, "keeping his covenant of Love to a thousand generations of those who love him and keep his commandments."[2]

The Lord had already established a covenant with Israel forty years earlier at Mount Horeb, when the mountain was covered in flashing lightning and booming thunder, and most terrifying of all, the voice of the Lord speaking out of the deep and dreadful darkness—at that time God also made a covenant with Israel. The Lord promised them, "'If you obey me fully and keep my covenant [the Ten Commandments], then out of all nations you will be my treasured possession. Although the whole earth is mine, you will be for me a kingdom of priests and a holy nation.' The people all responded together, 'We will do everything the Lord has said.'" Twice more they made this promise: "We will do everything the Lord has said. We will obey." And Moses took blood from a sacrifice on the altar and sprinkled it on the people, saying, "This is the blood of the covenant that the Lord has made with you in accordance with all these words."[3]

However, that was forty years earlier, and Israel had already rebelled against God and broken his covenant many times since then. Before Moses died and Israel marched off to war in the Promised Land, the Lord wanted to renew his covenant with them. It would be a new beginning for them at a very important time in their history.

This was not a new covenant, but the old one made a second time. Remember that "Deuteronomy" comes from two Greek words: *deuteros* (second) and *nomos* (law). God's law was given twice to Israel. The first time was at Horeb, just after they left Egypt, and the second time was now in Moab, just before they entered Canaan. The Ten Commandments were the terms of God's covenant that he required his people to keep. Just as there was a second giving of the same law in Deuteronomy, there was also a second entering into the same covenant.

Sometimes a husband and wife, although they have never been separated, have a second wedding ceremony, when they renew their marriage vows to each other and again pledge themselves to be united to one another in love until death parts them. In a similar way God and the people of Israel repeated their covenant promises. The Lord again declared his promise that the Israelites would be his people, his treasured possession, and that he would protect them, provide for them, and promote them in every way. The people again declared their promise that the Lord would be their God, and that they would be faithful to him, obeying all his commandments. Earlier Moses said, "You have declared this day that the Lord is your God and that you will walk in his way, that you will keep his decrees, commands and laws, and that you will obey him. And the Lord has declared this day that you are his people, his treasured possession as he promised, and that you are to keep all his commands. He has declared that he will set you in praise, fame, and honour high above all the nations he has made and that you will be a people holy to the Lord your God, as he promised."[4] Then Moses and the priests said to all the people, "You have now become the people of the Lord your God."[5]

On the day that Moses renewed God's covenant with the people of Israel, there was no blazing, smoking, quaking mountain to fill the people with dread; there were no forks of lightning or bursts of thunder, and no terrifying voice speaking from the swirling darkness to make them tremble with fear. There was only the voice of Moses—a voice that would soon be silent—pleading with the people to believe the Lord and follow his commandments.

Moses reasoned with the people that they knew the Lord was God—their own eyes had seen the miraculous signs and wonders the Lord did for them in Egypt. And during those forty years of wandering in the wilderness, they had seen how God provided for them in a supernatural way. God said, "I did this so that you might know that I am the Lord your God!" But Moses despaired that all they had seen and heard was in vain. Moses said, "To this very day the Lord has not given you a mind that understands or eyes that see or ears that hear."[6] Many of them still did not believe that the Lord was God.

Moses was afraid that the Israelites would be enticed to worship other gods, becoming ensnared by the sin of idolatry, and breaking God's covenant. Moses warned the people, "You yourselves know how we lived in Egypt and how we passed through the countries on our way here. You saw among them their detestable images of wood and stone, their idols of silver and gold. Make sure there is no man or woman, clan or tribe among you today whose heart turns away from the Lord our God to go and worship the gods of those nations; make sure there is no root among you that produces such bitter poison."[7] Yes, idolatry would be a fatal poison. If it seeped into someone's heart, it would destroy that person; if it seeped into the heart of the nation, it would destroy the whole land.

Moses warned the people that they were not safe simply because they had entered into a covenant with God. If their hearts were far from God, if they secretly worshipped other gods, they must not think they were safe and blessed because they were part of Israel, God's covenant community. Moses warned such deceivers that the covenant did not protect them—it made their sin all the more serious. He warned also that their sin would spread, ruining not only themselves but the whole nation, bringing disaster on everyone.

If such a person had turned away from the Lord to worship other gods, Moses warned that "the Lord will never be willing to forgive him. God's wrath and zeal will burn against that man. All the curses written in this book will fall upon him, and the Lord will blot out his name from under heaven." Such a man would think this sin was a secret hidden deep in the darkness of his own heart, and that no one could know that he worshipped other gods, but Moses warned, "The Lord will single him out from all the tribes of Israel for disaster, according to all the curses of the covenant written in this book of the law."[8]

What would happen if whole tribes—or the whole nation—rebelled against the Lord and broke his covenant, forsaking the Lord and worshipping false, worthless idols—worthless though they were made of silver and gold? They would not be spared just because everyone was doing it. Moses warned that calamities would fall upon the whole land—it would no longer be a good green land, flowing with milk and honey. Moses said, "The whole land will be a burning waste of salt and sulphur—nothing planted, nothing sprouting, no vegetation growing on it. It will be like the destruction of Sodom and Gomorrah . . . which the Lord overthrew in his fierce anger." All the surrounding nations would be amazed at this destruction and ask, "Why has the Lord done this to the land? Why this fierce burning anger?" And the answer would be a sad and simple one: "It is because this people abandoned the covenant of the Lord, the God of their fathers, the covenant he made with them when he brought them out of Egypt. They went off and worshipped other gods and bowed down to them, gods they did not know, gods he had not given them. Therefore the Lord's anger burned against this land, so that he brought on it all the curses written in this book. In furious anger and in great wrath the Lord uprooted them from their land and thrust them into another land."[9]

God revealed all these things to Israel through his servant Moses in the hearing of them all. Moses said, "The things revealed belong to us and to our children forever—that we may follow all the words of this law." The covenant was a blessing for them![10]

How blessed were the people of Israel! To them belonged the covenants, the laws of God, true worship, and all the promises, especially the great promise of the Messiah! One day that Messiah would be the mediator of a new covenant in his own precious blood, but until that day arrived Israel must be careful to keep the old covenant and make sure that no one had an unbelieving heart that turned away from the living God.[11]

LESSON 8: TEACHER'S GUIDE

Renewal of the Covenant

VISUAL AIDS:

Photos of wedding ceremonies from around the world would be useful for this lesson. This can spark a good discussion on the nature of a covenant.

MEMORY WORK:

> "Know therefore that the Lord your God is God. He is the faithful God keeping his covenant of Love to a thousand generations of those who love him and keep his commandments."
>
> Deuteronomy 7:9

REVIEW QUESTIONS:

1. Moses summoned the Israelites to come before the Lord. Who was required to attend this meeting?
2. What was happening that Moses called the whole community of Israel to stand before the Lord?
3. What did God promise as part of this covenant? What did the people promise? What part did Moses play in this covenant renewal?
4. When and where had the Lord had already established a covenant with Israel?
5. Was the covenant in Deuteronomy a new covenant?
6. Why did God want to renew the old covenant with Israel at this time?
7. How did the Israelites know that the Lord was really God? What had their own eyes witnessed?

8. What was the "bitter poison" about which Moses warned the people?
9. Some people thought they were safe and blessed—even if they didn't believe in God—because they were part of the covenant community. Did the covenant protect them in their sin? What would happen to them if they did not repent, but persisted in their rebellion against God? Do you think there are people like that in the church? Are they safe in their unbelief, simply because they go to church, have been baptized, listen to the preaching, take the Lord's Supper, or sing in the choir?

PRAYER:

Our heavenly Father, we thank you for loving us enough to make a covenant with us and for loving us enough to send your Son Jesus into this world to make a new covenant with us in his own precious blood. O Lord, let not the bitter root of unbelief spring up to poison our hearts, but let our hearts be faithful to you, ever rejoicing in your Love, ever believing your Word. Help us to love you with all our hearts!

PSALMS TO SING:

There are many songs about God's covenant:

25C . . . and 21BD; 32D; 44CE; 50AC; 78BD; 103C; 105A; 111AB; 115C

Lesson 9

A TALE OF TWO MOUNTAINS

- Deuteronomy 27; 11:26–32;
- Joshua 8:30–35

On the other side of the Jordan River, in the middle of the Promised Land, two rocky mountains stood side by side. Perhaps the Israelites could already see the peaks of those two mountains in the distance as they gazed across the river towards the land God had promised them, for Moses said, "As you know, these mountains are across the Jordan River, westward, toward the setting sun." Moses wanted to make sure the Israelites knew exactly where these mountains were located. He told them that these mountains stood near a famous forest of tall trees, "near the great trees of Moreh, in the territory of the Canaanites," in a region called the Arabah in the vicinity of a town called Gilgal.[1]

Why did the Israelites need to know exactly where these mountains were? They did not look important—they were just bare mountains. In fact, they looked as if God had "shorn" them of any vegetation, as a man would sheer the wool off a sheep. Nothing grew there—no leafy trees, no bright flowers, no lush grasses. In fact, the name of one mountain (Mount Ebal) meant "bare" and the name of the other mountain (Mount Gerazim) meant "waste." But God was going to have the Israelites plant something very important on these mountains.

Moses and the elders of Israel commanded the people, "When you have crossed the Jordan River into the land the Lord your God is giving you, set up some large stones and coat them with plaster. Write on them all the words of this law. . . . And when you have crossed the Jordan River, set up these stones on Mount Ebal. . . . And you shall write very clearly all the words of this law on these stones you have set up."[2] On that bare mountain in the heart of the land, they would be planting the law of the Lord. Those stones standing on the mountain would help the Israelites to remember to keep all of God's laws. Mount Ebal was no longer Mount Bare—a barren place on the face of the earth. The Word of the Lord was planted there!

There was something else that must be planted on that bare rocky mountain—more rocks. Moses commanded, "Build there an altar to the Lord your God, an altar of stones. Do not use any iron tool upon them. Build the altar to the Lord your God with field stones."[3] God commanded the Israelites to use just ordinary stones that they found in the fields. The stones were not to be carved with designs or shaped by any man using any kind of tool. God's altar was to be a heap of plain, uncut, unadorned stones.

That day on the mountain, when they set up the stones with God's commandments and when they built the stone altar for God's sacrifices, there was to be a worship service—a holy convocation and celebration, when all Israel rejoiced in the presence of the Lord their God. Sacrificing, worshipping, rejoicing—it was all part of the holy life that God's people must live. Not only did barren Mount Ebal now have the Word of the Lord planted on it, it was also covered with people who were praying, singing, and praising God. It was a holy place to worship the one true God. Mount Ebal had become a place of significance in heaven and on earth.

There was yet another thing that the Israelites must plant on those two bare mountains, but this time they must plant it with their voices rather than their hands. When they crossed the Jordan River, all the Israelites must stand on those two mountains and proclaim the blessings and the curses of the covenant. Six of the twelve tribes must stand on Mount Gerizim to proclaim the blessings; the other six tribes must stand on Mount

Ebal to proclaim the curses. Moses said, "See, I am setting before you today a blessing and a curse—the blessing if you obey the commands of the Lord your God, . . . the curse if you disobey the commands of the Lord your God and turn from the way that I commanded you today by following other gods, which you have not known."[4] Mount Gerizim would no longer be known for being a wasteland—it would be known for the blessings pronounced upon it.

It was the usual work of the priests to bless the Israelites. They daily pronounced this blessing upon the people: "The LORD bless you and keep you; the LORD make his face shine upon you and be gracious to you; the LORD turn his face toward you and give you peace."[5] And on that day, when they assembled on the two mountains in the Promised Land, perhaps the priests would again pronounce that blessing upon the people. Then perhaps there would be a thunderous response as the Israelites on Mount Gerizim shouted their joyous "Amen!" to God's blessing. But we do not know, for all that we see recorded in the Scriptures were the curses that the priests were commanded to pronounce upon all who violated God's holy law.

Moses commanded the Levites (the tribe chosen to be priests) to recite to all the people of Israel in one loud voice the curses that would befall anyone who broke the law of God. There were twelve curses in all. The first curse proclaimed by the priests would be against anyone who broke the first two commandments: "Cursed is the man who carves an image or casts an idol—the work of a craftsman's hands and a thing detestable to the Lord—and who sets it up in secret."[6] Then all the people, all who stood on Mount Ebal, would confirm this curse with their own voices, shouting, "Amen!"

Curse after curse was to be pronounced by the priests against anyone who disobeyed the law of the Lord. Idolaters, murderers, adulterers—they all were cursed by the priests. Twelve times the priests would pronounce a curse. Twelve times the people would shout in unison, "Amen!" The final curse was all-inclusive, the net that would catch us all: "Cursed is the man who does not uphold the words of this law by carrying them out." And one final time the people would shout, "Amen!" What a solemn warning that would be (and hopefully not soon forgotten) when all the priests of Israel in one loud voice thundered God's curses, and when all the people standing on the mountain responded in an even louder voice, "AMEN!"

If one had ears to hear and eyes to see, Mount Ebal and Mount Gerizim would no longer be barren wastelands with nothing but the lonely sound of the wind moaning among the rocks. Instead, if one looked with the eyes of faith, the rocky land would sprout blessings like flowers and curses like thistles. And in the sound of the wind, one listening with the ears of faith could hear the Word of God and the "Amen! Amen!" of the people echoing around those mountains forever.

The Tale of One More Mountain

In the accounts of the events on Mount Ebal and Mount Gerizim, a record of the blessings is strangely absent. We hear only the curses. But when Jesus Christ came to this earth, he came with blessings rather than curses.[7] Like the priests long ago, Jesus—our great high priest—also went up on a mountainside and there he delivered his most famous sermon, known as the Sermon on the Mount. From this mountain Jesus proclaimed The Beatitudes—the blessings.[8] It was as if Israel had to wait hundreds of years to hear the blessings proclaimed from the mountain. But when those blessings finally came, they were pronounced from the lips of their promised Saviour. He had the blessed words of eternal life. The law of Moses condemned men, but the gospel of Christ saved them.

The law of Moses put men under a curse, but Christ redeemed us from the curse of the law, so that we might receive the promised blessing by faith.[9] "From the fullness of his grace we have all received blessing upon blessing. For the law was given through Moses, but grace and truth came through Jesus Christ."[10] It is in Christ that we are blessed and blessed again with every spiritual blessing to the praise of God's glorious grace.[11] Amen!

LESSON 9: TEACHER'S GUIDE

A Tale of Two Mountains

VISUAL AIDS:

Photographs of Mount Ebal and Mount Gerizim, or any picture of two bare rocky mountains, would be useful for this lesson. You could also show your students Mount Ebal and Mount Gerizim on a map of ancient Israel.

MEMORY WORK:

"The law was given through Moses; grace and truth came through Jesus Christ."

John 1:17

"From the fullness of his grace we have all received blessing upon blessing."

John 1:16

REVIEW QUESTIONS:

1. Two rocky mountains stood side by side in the Promised Land. Describe how those mountains looked. What were their names? What did their names mean?
2. What two things did God command the Israelites to "plant" on Mount Ebal? What purpose did they serve?
3. God commanded six tribes of Israel to stand on one mountain and face the remaining six tribes standing on the other mountain, with the priests standing in between. What did the people who stood on Mount Ebal do? What did the people who stood on Mount Gerizim do? What did the priests do?
4. Why did God command Israel to do this?

5. What was the first curse the priests pronounced? What was the last curse they pronounced?
6. When Jesus, our great high priest, preached in the land of Israel, he also spoke on a mountain. What do we call this sermon? What do we call the blessings he pronounced?
7. How can we escape the curse of the law, and the curse of sin and death? How can we be blessed?

PRAYER:

Dear God, thank you for the Sermon on the Mount, and for Jesus' words of blessing, not cursing. Help us to live blessed lives, trusting in our Saviour day by day. Deliver us from evil, and forgive all our sins. Amen.

PSALMS TO SING:

These psalms are all filled with resounding amens: "Amen, amen, forevermore. Amen, amen, forevermore" (72C).

72C (11, 12) . . . and 41C; 72D; 89I; 106G

The mountains and hills often find a place in the songs of Zion: "Let the mountains sing together and rejoice before the Lord" (Psalm 98).

98AB . . . and 46ABC; 65B (4, 6); 95A; 95C (1–3); 97A; 104AE;
114; 121ABC; 125 (1, 2); 144A (1–4); 148

BLESSING OR CURSING

• Deuteronomy 28

Once the Israelites were settled in the Promised Land, the people would remember the Word of the Lord whenever they looked towards Mount Ebal and Mount Gerizim, which could be seen from a great distance away. The geography of the land itself would constantly present their options: blessing if they kept the covenant by obedience, cursing if they broke the covenant by disobedience. That choice would always be before their eyes.

The Blessings of the Covenant (Deuteronomy 28:1–14)

What were the covenant blessings that God would shower on his people? Moses said, "If you fully obey the Lord your God and carefully follow all his commands I give you today, the Lord your God will set you high above all the nations on earth. All these blessings will come upon you and accompany you if you obey the Lord your God. You will be blessed in the city and blessed in the country. The fruit of your womb will be blessed, and the crops of your land and the young of your livestock—the calves of your herds and the lambs of your flocks. Your basket and your kneading trough will be blessed. You will be blessed when you come in and blessed when you go out." They would be blessed everywhere in every time in every way and in everything! Wherever they lived and wherever they went, from the time they were born until the time they died, they would be blessed.

They would be blessed with prosperity.

Moses said, "The Lord will open the heavens, the storehouse of his bounty, to send rain on your land in season and to bless all the work of your hands. The Lord will grant you abundant prosperity!" Their farms would flourish, yielding an abundance of food. Even their barns would be blessed—filled with the produce of their land. Their baskets would be filled with bread and fruit; their plates would be filled with the most delicious and nutritious of foods. Israel would be a wealthy nation because of God's blessing. Moses said, "You will lend to many nations, but will borrow from none. The Lord will make you the head, not the tail."

They would be blessed with a healthy and increasing population. The Israelites would be a healthy people; they would be well and strong and the Lord would bless them with growing numbers of children and make them into a great nation, just as he promised. Their homes would be filled with the life and laughter of children and grandchildren. "The fruit of your womb will be blessed."

They would be blessed with victory and security.

Moses said, "The Lord will grant that the enemies who rise up against you will be defeated before you. They will come at you from one direction, but flee from you in seven." Israel would be free from the tyranny of foreign nations. Israel would be established as a world power. Moses said, "If you pay attention to the commands of the Lord your God that I give you this day and carefully follow them, you will always be at the top, never at the bottom!"

All these blessings God would shower on his people if they loved and obeyed him with all their heart. However, they could expect exactly the opposite if they neglected the commands of the Lord!

The Curses of the Covenant (Deuteronomy 28:15–68)

What were the curses of the covenant that God would bring on his people? Moses said, "If you do not obey the Lord your God and do not carefully follow all his commands and decrees I am giving you today, all these curses will come upon you and overtake you. You will be cursed in the city and cursed in the country. Your basket and kneading trough will be cursed. The fruit of your womb will be cursed, and the crops of your land, and the calves of your herds and the lambs of your flocks. You will be cursed when you come in and cursed when you go out."

If Israel broke the covenant and did not keep the commands, there was nowhere they could hide from God's curses. Wherever they fled, whatever they did, God's curses would overtake them. Moses said, "The Lord will send on you curses, confusion, and rebuke in everything you put your hand to, until you are destroyed and come to sudden ruin because of the evil you have done in forsaking him. You will be unsuccessful in everything you do."

Instead of prosperity, they would be cursed with poverty. Israel would become the least of all nations, the lowest of all peoples. While other peoples rose higher and higher, they would "sink lower and lower" becoming "a thing of horror and an object of ridicule to all the nations." Instead of being the head, Moses warned, "you will be the tail."

Their crops would wither in the drought and shrivel up from disease. The sky would be hardened against them, yielding no rain; and the earth would be hardened against them, yielding no food. Moses said, "The Lord will strike you with . . . scorching heat and drought, with blight and mildew, which will plague you until you perish. The sky over your head will be bronze, the ground beneath you iron. The Lord will turn the rain of your country into dust and powder; it will come down from the skies until you are destroyed."

Their land and their crops would be plagued with pests. Moses said, "You will sow much seed in the field but the harvest will be little, because locusts will devour it. You will plant vineyards and cultivate them, but you will not drink the wine or gather the grapes, because worms will eat them. You will have olive trees throughout your country but you will not use the oil, because the olives will drop off. Swarms of locusts will take over all your trees and the crops of your land."

Their enemies would gobble up everything they owned. Moses said, "A people that you do not know will eat what your land and labour produce, and you will have nothing but cruel oppression all your days. . . . The Lord will bring a nation against you from far away, from the ends of the earth, like an eagle swooping down, a nation whose language you will not understand, a fierce-looking nation without respect for the old or pity for the young"— a nation who would not care if little Israelite children starved to death. Moses said, "They will devour the young of your livestock and the crops of your land until you are destroyed. They will leave you no grain, new wine or oil, nor any calves of your herds of lambs of your flocks until you are ruined! . . . Day after day you will be oppressed and robbed, with no one to rescue you."

Everyone they loved and everything they owned would be taken from them. Moses said, "You will be pledged to be married to a woman, but another will take her. You will build a house, but you will not live in it. You will plant a vineyard, but you will not even begin to enjoy its fruit. Your ox will be slaughtered before your eyes, but you will eat none of it. your donkey will be forcibly taken from you and will not be returned. Your sheep will be given to your enemies, and no one will rescue them."

Everything would be stolen from them: their homes and farms, their flocks and herds, their gold and silver—and even their children, who were more precious to them than anything else. Moses said, "Your sons and daughters will be given to another nation, and you will wear out your eyes watching for them day after day, powerless to lift a hand. . . . You will have sons and daughters, but you will not keep them, because they will go into captivity."

Instead of health and an increasing population, they would be cursed with disease. Moses warned, "The Lord will plague you with diseases until he has destroyed you from the land you are entering to possess. The Lord will strike you with wasting disease, with fever and inflammation . . . which will plague you until you perish. . . . The Lord will afflict you with the boils of Egypt and with tumours, festering sores and the itch, from which you cannot be cured. The Lord will afflict you with madness, blindness, and confusion of mind. . . . The sights you see will drive you mad! The Lord will afflict your knees and legs with painful boils that cannot be cured, spreading from the soles of your feet to the top of your head."

Moses warned the people, "If you do not carefully follow all the words of this law, which are written in this book, and do not revere this glorious and awesome name—the Lord your God—the Lord will send fearful plagues on you and your descendants, harsh and prolonged disasters, and severe and lingering illnesses. He will bring upon you all the diseases of Egypt that you dreaded, and they will cling to you. . . . Just as it pleased the Lord to make you prosper and increase in number, so it will please him to ruin and destroy you."

Instead of victory and security, they would be cursed with oppression and destruction. Their protection from God would be gone. Foreign enemies would defeat, destroy, and enslave them. The Lord had delivered them from bondage, but he would send them back again into a state of cruel affliction and oppression.

Moses said, "The Lord will cause you to be defeated before your enemies. You will come at them from one direction, but flee from them in seven—and you will become a thing of horror to all the kingdoms of the earth." Their bodies would cover the ground, to be devoured by scavengers. There would be no burial and no one to weep or mourn over their destruction.

Moses warned that the Lord would bring foreign nations against them from far away: "They will lay siege to all the cities throughout your land until the high fortified walls in which you trust fall down. They will besiege all the cities throughout the land the Lord your God is giving you. . . . You will be uprooted from the land you are entering to possess. Then the Lord will scatter you among all nations, from one end of the earth to the other. Among those nations you will find no repose, no resting place for the sole of your foot. There the Lord will give you an anxious mind, eyes weary with longing, and a despairing heart. You will live in constant suspense, filled with dread both day and night, never sure of your life." It would be a terrible time in Israel.

A Warning to Future Generations

Moses said, "Your children who follow you in later generations and foreigners who come from distant lands—they will see the calamities that have fallen on the land and the diseases with which the Lord has afflicted it. All the nations will ask, 'Why has the Lord done this to this land? Why this fierce, burning anger?' And the answer will be, 'It is because this people abandoned the covenant of the Lord, the God of their fathers, the covenant he made with them when he brought them out of Egypt. They went off and worshipped other gods and bowed down to them—gods they did not know, gods he had not given them. Therefore the Lord's anger burned against this land, so that he brought on it all the curses written in this book. In furious anger and in great wrath the Lord uprooted them from their land and thrust them into another land.'"[1]

"All these curses will come upon you," warned Moses. "They will pursue you and overtake you until you are destroyed, because you did not obey the Lord your God and observe the commands and decrees he gave you. They will be a sign and a wonder to you and your descendants forever. Because you did not serve the Lord your God joyfully and gladly in the time of prosperity, therefore in hunger and thirst, in nakedness and dire poverty, you will serve the enemies the Lord sends against you. He will put an iron yoke on your neck, until he has destroyed you!"

Punishment and Restoration

With all these words Moses warned the people what would happen in the future—not merely what might happen, but what would happen if they forsook the Lord—so that they would fear the Lord and follow all the words of the law in the book of Deuteronomy.

Would these terrible things happen? Would the Israelites forsake the Lord, bringing all these calamities upon them? Sadly, yes. As we read through the rest of the Bible, we see that the word of the Lord did not fail. God brought them into the land as he promised—and when Israel forsook their God, he uprooted them from the land as he promised.

What would happen if the Israelites turned back to the Lord when they were exiled in a foreign land? Moses said, "When all these blessings and curses I have set before you come upon you and you take them to heart wherever the Lord your God disperses you among the nations, and when you and your children return to the Lord your God and obey him with all your heart and all your soul according to everything I command you today, then the Lord your God will restore your fortunes and he will have compassion on you and he will gather you again from all the nations where he has scattered you. Even if you have been banished to the most distant land under the heavens, from there the Lord your God will gather you and bring you back. . . . The Lord your God will circumcise your hearts and the hearts of your descendants, so that you may love him with all your heart and with all your soul, and live. The Lord your God will put all these curses on your enemies who hate and persecute you. The Lord will again delight in you and make you prosperous, just as he delighted in your fathers, if you obey the Lord your God and keep his commands and decrees that are written in this book of the law and turn to the Lord your God with all your heart and with all your soul."[2]

The Lord made very clear what would be the result of obedience, and what would be the result of disobedience. With his last words, Moses encouraged Israel to choose the blessings of obedience and keep the covenant of the Lord. He said, "Now what I am commanding you today is not too difficult for you or beyond your reach. No, the word is very near you. It is in your mouth and in your heart so you may obey it."[3]

LESSON 10: TEACHER'S GUIDE

Blessing or Cursing

VISUAL AIDS:

Collect all kinds of photographs and have the children make two large collages—one picturing a blessed life and land, the other picturing a cursed life and land. Label one collage BLESSED and the other CURSED.

MEMORY WORK:

"May your unfailing Love rest upon us, O Lord, even as we put our hope in you."

Psalm 33:22

REVIEW QUESTIONS

1. What are the three main ways God would bless Israel if they kept his covenant?
2. How would God curse Israel with poverty and starvation if they broke his covenant?
3. How would God cause their population to decrease if they broke his covenant?
4. How would God take away their security if they broke his covenant?
5. If Israel persisted in rebellion against the Lord, what would God finally do to them?
6. If they repented and turned to the Lord again, what was God's promise?
7. What does the history of the nation of Israel show us about God's Word? What can we learn from their history that will help us in our lives?

PRAYER:

Our loving heavenly Father, keep us close to you. May we never stray from you or your Word, forsaking you or rejecting your holy laws. Help us, O Lord! Deliver us from evil. Rescue us from the evil one who leads the whole world astray. May your Holy Spirit lead us into all truth and protect us from all harm. Forgive our sins and bless our lives. Thank you for your promise, Lord Jesus, that you will never leave us or forsake us. Amen.

PSALMS TO SING:

The psalter is a book filled with the contrast between the righteous and the wicked—those who are blessed and those who are cursed.

37C . . . and 1AB; 5AB; 7A (5); 9A; 11; 32B (9, 12, 13); 32D (5); 33B; 34ABCDE; 36B; 37ABCDEF; 52AB; 55BC; 56; 58AB; 64AB; 68A; 73C; 75; 91A; 92ABC; 94AB; 104E; 109ABC; 112AB; 119P; 125; 138AB; 140AB; 142; 143ABC; 145C

These are psalms about the Lord being the judge of all the earth.

98AB . . . and 7AB; 9A; 50A; 67AB; 94A; 96B

Lesson 11

A CHOICE

• Deuteronomy 30:11–20

The Choice in the Garden

Long ago, when the Lord God made the heavens and the earth, he planted the Garden of Eden for the first two people he created. In that garden God made all kinds of wonderful trees grow out of the ground—trees that were exceptionally beautiful and bountiful, with graceful branches covered in green and gold and red leaves shimmering in the sunlight; trees adorned with fragrant blossoms that filled the air with a sweet intoxicating scent; trees that were laden with every kind of exotic fruit that would delight and sustain God's beloved human creatures.

In the middle of that beautiful grove were two very special trees that God had formed and named. One was called the Tree of Life and the other was called the Tree of the Knowledge of Good and Evil. With those two trees came a choice—and a commandment. The Lord God said to the man he made, "You are free to eat from any tree in the garden; but you must not eat from the Tree of the Knowledge of Good and Evil, for when you eat of it you will surely die."[1]

Those two trees in the middle of the garden represented a choice: life or death. If the first man and woman obeyed God, they would live; but if they disobeyed God, they would surely die. We know the tragic choice that they made. They broke God's commandment.[2]

And the Lord God banished the man from the Garden of Eden saying, "He must not be allowed to reach out his hand and take also from the Tree of Life and eat, and so live forever." After God drove the man out of the garden, he placed angels and a flaming sword flashing back and forth to guard the way to the Tree of Life.[3] The first human beings had chosen sin and death. Eternal life was now beyond their reach, an option they were no longer free to choose for themselves.

The Choice in the Promised Land

Thousands of years passed. God's people were camped beside the Jordan River, and beyond its rippling blue waters lay the Promised Land. Soon the Israelites would cross the river and begin to fight for the land that God had promised to them. And very soon Moses would die. But before he died, he left the Israelites with a very important choice. Perhaps they could see that choice beyond the Jordan River, far in the distance, represented by the peaks of Mount Ebal and Mount Gerazim.

Moses set before the Israelites life and death—life and all the goodness that would prosper them, or death and all the evil that would destroy them. It was a very clear choice and surely not a difficult one to decide which option to take. Moses said, "See, I set before you today life and prosperity, death and destruction. For I command you today to love the Lord your God, to walk in his ways, and to keep his commands, decrees, and laws; then you will live and increase, and the Lord your God will bless you in the land you are entering to possess. But if your heart turns away and you are not obedient and if you are drawn away to bow down to other gods and worship them, I declare to you this day that you will certainly be destroyed. You will not live long in the land you are crossing the Jordan River to enter and possess."[4]

Moses solemnly declared to the people that he had clearly set before them the choice between life and death, telling them, "This day I call heaven and earth as witnesses against you that I have set before you life and death, blessings and curses." Moses pleaded with the people to make the right choice. He said, "Now choose life, so that you and your children may live and that you may love the Lord your God, listen to his voice, and hold fast to him. For the Lord is your life!"[5] They were to choose to love God and to listen to his voice and to never let go of him. They were to cling to God the way people cling to their lives, because the Lord was their life.

Moses said, "Now what I am commanding you today is not too difficult for you or beyond your reach." What an amazing statement. To choose life was not beyond their reach! They were being given a real choice by God—another opportunity to choose life. The Tree of Life, "in the paradise of God,"[6] was inaccessible, guarded by angels and the flaming sword of the Lord—but Moses was offering them a choice on earth. He said, "It is not up in heaven . . . nor is it beyond the sea." It was right there, offered to them that very day, and not beyond their reach. "The word is very near you. It is in your mouth and in your heart so you may obey it," Moses told the people.

God had revealed his word, his law, to Israel. It was not hidden within the highest heavens or buried beyond the farthest oceans so that it was out of their reach. God's law wasn't just written on the stone tablets locked in the ark of the covenant, it was written upon their very hearts and lips. That is how near God's Word was to them!

The people knew what they must do to choose life—and it had to do with their own hearts. Again and again Moses had said to them, "Love the Lord your God with all your heart and with all your soul and with all your strength. Carefully observe all these commands I am giving you to follow—to love the Lord your God, to walk in all his ways and to hold fast to him. Turn to the Lord your God with all your heart and with all your soul. . . . Love him with all your heart and with all your soul—and live!"[7]

Reminders of the Choice

In the beginning, the first man and woman could look at the two beautiful trees in the middle of the Garden of Eden and see before them a choice: life or death. And thousands of years ago, when the ancient Israelites lived in the Promised Land, they could look at two rocky mountains and they also could see before them a choice: life or death, blessing or cursing. Today we also have a choice of life or death—but we live in many different countries of the world. Where can we look to remind us of that choice?

In our minds we must see a bare, rocky hill called The Skull (or Golgotha); and on that hill stand three very strange and ugly trees, without leaves, blossoms, or fruit—dead wood with just one branch on each tree crossing the main trunk. These three "trees" are crosses—Roman instruments of torture and execution upon which criminals were either tied or nailed. Then the crosses were lifted up, planted in the ground like trees, and the condemned men were left to hang there until they died. It was an excruciating death. And it is there we must look to see our choice: life or death, blessing or cursing.

Nailed to the middle cross we see a man who was not a criminal; in fact, he was the holy Son of God, not only a man who had committed no crime, but a man who had committed no sin. Signs were often nailed to the crosses, stating each man's name and crime. On this middle cross the sign read: Jesus of Nazareth, the King of the Jews. But if he was the Son of God and the King of the Jews, why was he hanging on a cross? And that was exactly what the people passing by the Place of the Skull or loitering around the execution ground said to Christ. "If you are the Son of God, come down from the cross! Save yourself! Then we will believe in you!" Even the robbers who hung on the crosses beside Jesus hurled insults at him, though they were dying men too.

It is at these two crosses bearing the two criminals that we must look to clearly see the choice that is before each one of us today. They clearly represent our choice: belief or unbelief, acceptance of Christ or rejection of Christ, eternal life or eternal death. As that dark day of death slowly progressed, one of the criminals continued heaping abuse upon the innocent man beside him. He used the last of his strength and the last of his breath to join the others in mocking Jesus. "Aren't you the Christ?" he sneered. "Save yourself and us!"

But the other criminal, dying on the other side of Jesus, was changing. His heart was turning towards God now, as his life was slipping away from him. He no longer joined his friend's mockery, but rebuked his hard-heartedness saying, "Don't you fear God, since you are under the same sentence? We are punished justly, for we are getting what our deeds deserve. But this man has done nothing wrong." Then he said something which showed that he believed that Jesus was the Son of God. He said,

"Jesus, remember me when you come into your kingdom." And Jesus answered this man, who had led a life of sin, but who had turned to him in faith, "I tell you the truth, today you will be with me in paradise."[8]

And so that man passed from death to life when he believed in Jesus. Later that day he died on his cross, but nevertheless he lived, for God had granted him eternal life.[9] "Because of his great Love for us, God, who is rich in mercy, made us alive with Christ, even when we were dead in sins. For it is by grace you have been saved, through faith, and this not from yourselves—it is the gift of God."[10]

When we look with our spiritual eyes at those three crosses planted on Golgotha, we must remember the choice that is always before us. We can be like the thief who doubted Christ, denying and disbelieving him to our own death and doom. The alternative is to be like the other thief, and come to Jesus believing in him and his power as the Son of God to raise us from the dead; we can recognise our sinfulness and worthlessness, and ask him to remember us and deliver us into his blessed kingdom.

Jesus said this about himself and his crucifixion: "The Son of Man must be lifted up, that everyone who believes in him may have eternal life. For God so loved the world that he gave his one and only Son, that whoever believes in him shall not perish but have eternal life. For God did not send his Son into the world to condemn the world, but to save the world through him. Whoever believes in him is not condemned, but whoever does not believe stands condemned already because he has not believed in the name of God's one and only Son."[11]

Our Choice Today

This is every person's own choice: life or death, to believe in Jesus or to not believe in Jesus, eternal life or eternal death. Again and again the Son of God set this choice before the people saying, "I tell you the truth: whoever hears my word and believes him who sent me has eternal life and will not be condemned; he has crossed over from death to life. Everyone who looks to the Son and believes in him shall have eternal life. I tell you the truth; he who believes has everlasting life."[12]

What must you do to gain eternal life? Remember what Moses said. The answer "is not too difficult for you or beyond your reach. It is not up in heaven, so that you have to ask, 'Who will ascend into heaven to get it and proclaim it to us, so that we may obey it?'"[13] For Christ himself came down from heaven to proclaim the way to us.[14] And the answer is not buried in the bowels of the earth or the depths of the sea. Christ died and descended into hell—the deepest darkest place in the universe—and then he was raised from the dead. He came back to life to give us the answer, and it was the same command: "How foolish you are and slow of heart to believe. Stop doubting and believe!"[15]

To believe in Jesus, the Son of God—is that command too difficult for us or beyond our reach? As Moses would answer, "No! The word is very near you; it is in your mouth and in your heart, so you may obey it"[16]—that is, the word of faith that we are proclaiming, "That if you confess with your mouth, 'Jesus is Lord' and believe in your heart that God raised him from the dead, you will be saved. For it is with your heart that you believe and are justified, and it is with your mouth that you confess and are saved. For everyone who calls on the name of the Lord will be saved."[17] That is God's promise to us, just as it was to the thief on the cross, who Christ said would be with him in paradise that very day.

Dear children, believe in the Lord Jesus Christ with your hearts and confess with your lips that he is the Son of God—and be saved. Dear children, remember the words of Moses: "Choose life . . . so that you may live!"

LESSON 11: TEACHER'S GUIDE

A Choice

VISUAL AIDS:

There are many photographs of beautiful trees from all over the world. They stand in stark contrast to the three "trees" planted on Golgotha—this scene is the subject of many drawings and paintings as well. Show your children some of these photos and pictures.

MEMORY WORK:

> Moses said, "I have set before you life and death, blessings and curses. Now choose life, so that you and your children may live and that you may love the Lord your God, listen to his voice, and hold fast to him. For the Lord is your life."
>
> Deuteronomy 30:19–20

> Jesus said, "I am the resurrection and the life. He who believes in me will live, even though he dies; and whoever lives and believes in me will never die."
>
> John 11:25–26

REVIEW QUESTIONS:

1. What were the names of the two trees in the centre of the Garden of Eden? What did God command about them?
2. What choice did those two trees represent? What did the first man and woman choose? What was the result?
3. Moses gave the Israelites a choice. What was it? What did Moses urge them to choose?
4. Was what Moses commanded them too difficult? How close was God's Word to them?

5. We also have a choice. What must we see that will represent that choice clearly to us?
6. What kind of "trees" did the Romans plant in Jesus' day? How did they use these trees?
7. What did the people say as Jesus hung dying on the cross?
8. Who was crucified with Jesus? Where were their crosses planted?
9. What did the two thieves say to Jesus? When they died, how were their two deaths different?
10. How can we escape from death and have eternal life?

PRAYER:

Our merciful heavenly Father, you have graciously offered us life. Let us not be dull and undiscerning; let us not be wicked and unbelieving. Rather, let us choose wisely and believe in your only Son, whom you sent from heaven, who died on the cross for our sakes, that we might live. O Lord, may we never reject the Love of such a great Saviour! May our hearts always trust him and love him; may our lips always confess that Jesus is Lord, with our voices singing his praises forever and ever. Amen.

PSALMS TO SING:

These are songs about the King—songs of praise for our great King Jesus!

145A . . . and 2; 5AB; 21A; 24ABC; 28A (6–8); 29A (1, 6);
45A; 47A; 89D; 95A; 96B; 98AB; 99C; 103D; 136A (1, 2);
146B (1, 7); 149

Lesson 12

A NEW LEADER

- Deuteronomy 31:1–8
- Numbers 27:12–23

"The Lord Goes with You"

As Israel was waiting for orders to cross the river and march into the Promised Land, Moses delivered some devastating news: he was about to die. Moses said, "I am now one hundred and twenty years old and I am no longer able to lead you."[1]

However, Israel would not be left without a leader to guide them across the river and to lead them into battle. Moses said, "The Lord your God himself will cross over ahead of you. He will destroy these nations before you, and you will take possession of their land. . . . The Lord will deliver them to you, and you must do to them all that I have commanded you. Be strong and courageous. Do not be afraid or terrified because of them, for the Lord your God goes with you. He will never leave you nor forsake you."[2]

The Israelites must follow their leader, the Lord, by faith. They must follow him across the river and into battle by faith, not by sight,—for they could not see the invisible God who would go before them and fight for them, but they would clearly be able to see their enemies. Therefore they must be strong and courageous, believing that God went with them.

Moses would soon be leaving them, and never again would they see his face or hear his voice—but God would never leave them or forsake them. Yes, Moses was dying, but he left them with words of great comfort: "The Lord your God goes with you. He will never leave you nor forsake you!"

Moses Asks for a Visible Leader

When the Israelites were camped on the edge of the Jordan River, the Lord had said to Moses, "Go up this mountain . . . and see the land I have given the Israelites. After you have seen it, you too will be gathered to your people. . . ." Moses had been concerned. What awaited the people on the other side of the Jordan River was war—who would lead the Israelites into battle? So Moses asked God to choose a new leader for them. He said, "May the Lord, the God of the spirits of all mankind, appoint a man over this community to go out and to come in before them, one who will lead them out and bring them in, so the Lord's people will not be like sheep with out a shepherd." So while the Lord had promised to lead the Israelites himself, Moses also left the Israelites another leader—a man like themselves, whom they could follow by sight. The Israelites could trust this man, for he had proved to be faithful all his life. His name was Joshua.

Joshua's Qualifications

Joshua had been Moses' aide since his youth.[3] He had witnessed everything that happened to Israel, and had seen how Moses handled every situation. During all those years with Moses, Joshua had been watching and listening; although he was Moses' servant, he had been in training to be Israel's next leader. And in every situation on their long journey, from the time he was a young man, Joshua had supported Moses when most of the people, even Moses' own brother and sister, had rebelled against him. He had been with Moses through good times and bad times—at the heights of glory and in the depths of despair. Joshua was with Moses when he climbed up the mountain of God to receive the Ten Commandments on the tablets of stone,[4] and he was also with Moses when they climbed down the mountain together and heard the sound of the people worshipping the golden calf.[5]

Because Joshua was close to Moses, he was also close to the Lord—a very important requirement for Israel's leader. Joshua went up the mountain of God with Moses and he went into the Lord's Tabernacle with Moses. He saw all the signs and wonders and miracles that God performed through Moses, and he saw the Lord's deliverance again and again.

Later in Israel's journey, whenever Moses entered the tent of meeting to speak with the Lord face to face, Joshua went with him—but when Moses returned to the camp to speak with the people, Joshua did not leave the Tabernacle; he stayed with the Lord. You see, Joshua himself was a man of faith and a man of prayer, who was no stranger to God.[6] As Israel's new leader Joshua knew that his help and strength were in the Lord.

Not only was Joshua close to the Lord, he was also a seasoned warrior who knew how to lead an army. He had been Israel's army commander from their very first military encounter in the wilderness against the Amalekites. It was the first enemy they had faced and fought. In that attack, Moses had lifted his hands in prayer, but it was Joshua who had lifted his hands in war. With sword in hand, Joshua distinguished himself as a great leader and led the Israelites to victory.[7]

Joshua was also one of twelve men whom Moses sent as spies to explore the Promised Land—but one of only two men who urged the people to take the land by trusting their God.[8] He showed faithfulness in this situation, and because he "followed the Lord wholeheartedly," God promised that Joshua would one day enter and possess the Promised Land, while the rest of Israel would perish in the desert.[9] Not only that, Joshua was given the privilege of assigning to each tribe their inheritance.[10]

"Joshua" was not the name his parents gave him at birth. For years his name had been "Hoshea" (salvation), but Moses changed his name to Joshua, which means, "the Lord is salvation."[11] It was a very significant name change for Israel's new leader. Joshua bore in himself (in his very name!) the reality that salvation was from the Lord—which the commander of Israel's army must never forget. In every battle he must remember that his hope and trust were in God.

Moses Commissions Joshua

The Lord had said to Moses that he would not enter the Promised Land. God said, "Look at the land with your own eyes, since you are not going to cross this Jordan. But commission Joshua, and encourage and strengthen him, for he will lead this people across and he will cause them to inherit the land that you will see."[12] So now Moses summoned Joshua to strengthen him and encourage him, according to the word of the Lord.

The Lord commanded Moses, "Take Joshua, son of Nun, a man in whom is the Spirit, and lay your hand on him. Have him stand before Eleazar the priest and the entire assembly and commission him in their presence. Give him some of your authority so the whole Israelite community will obey him." So Moses took Joshua and made him stand before Eleazar the priest and the whole assembly. Moses laid his hands on him and commissioned him.[13] Joshua was filled with the Spirit and filled with wisdom, and the Israelites listened to him, obeying the command of the Lord.[14]

Moses said to Joshua in the presence of all Israel, "Be strong and courageous, for you must go with this people into the land that the Lord swore to their forefathers to give them, and you must divide it among them as their inheritance." It was an awesome task for any man. How would Joshua be able to do this? Moses urged Joshua to trust in God: "The Lord himself goes before you and will be with you. He will never leave you nor forsake you. Do not be afraid. Do not be discouraged."[15] These were Joshua's final instructions from his very old and beloved master—that he must trust in the Lord, who would always be with him.

The Lord Commissions Joshua

Then the Lord said to Moses, "Now the day of your death is near. Call Joshua and present yourselves at the tent of meeting, where I will commission him." When Moses and Joshua presented themselves there, the Lord appeared at the Tabernacle in a pillar of cloud, and the cloud stood over the entrance to the tent. After speaking to Moses, the Lord gave this command to Joshua: "Be strong and courageous, for you will bring the Israelites into the land I promised them on oath, and I myself will be with you."[16] Joshua heard the voice of God himself, the master of his master, commanding him and commissioning him with the same words Moses had spoken: "Be strong and courageous." The Lord also comforted him and encouraged him with the words: "I myself will be with you."

Joshua was now ready to lead the Israelites across the Jordan River and into the Promised Land. He was ready to lead them into war, for his master Moses and his sovereign Lord had prepared him for that task, arming him for the day of battle not with swords, but with words. Joshua would march ahead of Israel's army with the sword of the Spirit—the Word of God. The Lord himself had spoken to Joshua, filling him with strength and courage and faith. Joshua would advance into enemy territory knowing for certain that God was with him. So Joshua became Israel's new leader—but Joshua's leader was the Lord God himself.

LESSON 12: TEACHER'S GUIDE

A New Leader

VISUAL AIDS:

Bring photos of inaugurations or coronations so the children can see how nations today celebrate new leaders, whether presidents or kings and queens.

MEMORY WORK:

"The Lord himself goes before you and will be with you. He will never leave you nor forsake you. Do not be afraid. Do not be discouraged."
Deuteronomy 31:8

Jesus said, "Surely I am with you always, to the very end of the age."
Matthew 28:20

REVIEW QUESTIONS:

1. What sad news did Moses give the Israelites?
2. What invisible leader must the Israelites follow by faith?
3. Who now would lead Israel into the Promised Land?
4. How did the Israelites know that Joshua would make a good leader? Name three things that qualified Joshua to lead.
5. Who chose Joshua?
6. Who named Joshua? What does his name mean?

PRAYER:

Heavenly Father, long ago the Israelites could be confident because you gave them a great leader—Joshua. But you have given us a greater Joshua—that is, Jesus. Lord, we thank you that there is salvation in no one else. We thank you that we can trust in him, and so be strong and courageous and unafraid. Lord, we thank you for his promise to us, that he will never leave us or forsake us.

PSALMS TO SING:

"Joshua" means "the Lord is salvation." Here are just a few of the many salvation psalms:

62A (1, 4, 5); 98B . . . and 20AB; 25AB; 27DE; 31C (11); 40F (8);
51BE;65A; 70ABC; 85A; 98A; 106A;116C; 118BC; 119WX

These following salvation songs can be sung to the tune of "Amazing Grace," stringing together verses from different psalms:

Psalms 3 (5); 13 (5); 37F (25, 26); 40D (14, 15); 118C (14, 17);
140A (6)

Lesson 13

A BOOK, A SONG, AND A BLESSING

• Deuteronomy 31–33

Before Moses died, he left the Israelites with three very important gifts: a book, a song, and a blessing.

A Book

Something of utmost importance that Moses did before he died was to make sure that his words—that is, God's Word—continued to live after him. Soon his voice would be silenced in death, but the Word of the Lord through him must continue to speak. Deuteronomy says, "Moses finished writing in a book the words of this law from beginning to end."[1] He preserved the Word of God that had been entrusted to him by writing it down and commanding that the book would be stored in a safe place.

The Ten Commandments were engraved on tablets of stone by the finger of Almighty God, but all the other commands of the Lord were written down on scrolls by the hand of Moses. And when he had finished the book, Moses gave this command to the Levites: "Take this book of the law and place it beside the ark of the covenant of the Lord your God. There it will remain."[2] The stone tablets with God's law were stored in the ark of the covenant, within the Holy of Holies in the Tabernacle, and the book of Deuteronomy was placed right next to them. There was no safer place in all of Israel to keep these words. Surely there they would not be lost or stolen or forgotten.

Then Moses carefully prescribed a regular reading schedule for this precious book. He told Israel when and where it was to be read; he told them who was to read it and who was to hear it; and he told them why it was to be read. Moses commanded the priests and the elders of Israel, "At the end of every seven years . . . during the Feast of Tabernacles, when all Israel comes to appear before the Lord your God at the place he will choose, you shall read this law before them in their hearing. Assemble the people—men, women, and children, and the aliens living in your towns—so they can listen and learn to fear the Lord your God and follow carefully all the words of this law. Their children, who do not know this law, must hear it and learn to fear the Lord your God as long as you live in the land."[3] This regular reading of God's law would ensure that it would always teach and rule Israel, even the succeeding generations of children not yet born.[4]

Moses would die and his remains would be lost forever, but he ensured that God's words through him would not be lost. Four thousand years later and many thousands of miles away, we are still reading copies of the book of the law that Moses wrote. His words have gone forth to the ends of the earth and have spanned the centuries right into this new millennium. Even good men like Moses die—"but the Word of our God endures forever."[5]

A Song

The Lord also gave Moses a song to teach to the Israelites. It was not a happy little song to cheer them up—it was a long and tragic song about how Israel would turn away from the God who loved them. After he had brought them into the land flowing with milk and honey, the people would turn to worship other gods, rejecting the Lord and breaking his covenant of Love. God knew beforehand what they would do—and this song was a witness for him against the Israelites. When many difficulties and disasters came upon them because of their sin, this song would testify against them.

God said to Moses, "You are going to rest with your fathers, and these people will soon prostitute themselves to the foreign gods of the land they are entering. They will forsake me and break the covenant I made with them. On that day I will become angry with them and forsake them; I will hide my face from them, and they will be destroyed . . . because of all their wickedness in turning to other gods. Now write down for yourselves this song and teach it to the Israelites and have them sing it, so that it may be a witness for me against them."[6]

Because this song was written in the book of Deuteronomy, it too was placed beside the ark of the covenant in the Holy of Holies in God's Tabernacle. Moses said, "There it will remain as a witness against you. For I know how rebellious and stiff-necked you are. If you have been rebellious against the Lord while I am still alive and with you, how much more will you rebel when I die! Assemble before me all the elders of your tribes, so that I can speak these words in their hearing and call heaven and earth to testify against them."[7] Then Moses recited the words of his song from beginning to end in the hearing of the whole assembly of Israel.

The song of Moses began with his hope and his plea that these last words of his teaching, which would be sung by all Israel, would not be in vain. He prayed that these words would not vanish with the sound of their singing, but would fall like rain and soak into the ground of their hard hearts, softening them and watering them with the word of truth, so that their faith and their love for God would grow:

> Listen, O heavens, and I will speak;
> Hear, O earth, the words of my mouth.
> Let my teaching fall like rain and my words descend like dew,
> Like showers on new grass, like abundant rain on tender plants.

This was a song about the Love of God. In it, Moses reminded the people yet again about everything God had done for them, and that God had loved them and cared for them as a father loves and cares for his children. "Is he not your Father, your Creator, who made you and formed you?" And he urged them to realize how gracious God had been in choosing Israel. "Remember the days of old; consider the generations long past."

They had been lost in the desert, a barren and howling wasteland—and God found them. He shielded them, guided them, carried them, and nourished them. In every way God had loved his people. Moses continued his song by praising God because of his goodness:

> I will proclaim the name of the Lord.
> Oh praise the greatness of our God! He is the Rock!
> His works are perfect and all his ways are just.
> A faithful God who does no wrong, upright and just is he.

How did Israel respond to God's greatness and love? Moses testified in his song against them, prophesying with certainty what would happen in the future. He spoke as if it had already happened:

> They made him jealous with their foreign gods
> And angered him with their detestable idols.
> They sacrificed to demons which are not God. . . .
> You deserted the Rock, who fathered you.
> You forgot the God who gave you birth.

They abandoned the God who made them and rejected the Lord who saved them. Moses asked the Israelites:

> Is this the way you repay the Lord,
> O foolish and unwise people?

Moses' sad song continued with God's righteous response:

> The Lord saw this and rejected them
> Because he was angered by his sons and daughters.
> "I will hide my face from them," [God] said,
> "And see what their end will be;
> For they are a perverse generation,
> Children who are unfaithful.
> They made me jealous by what is no god
> And angered me with their detestable idols. . . .
> [So] I will heap calamities upon them."

God warned that the fire of his anger had been kindled. Because Israel refused to be ruled by the Lord, his law, and his Love, they would experience another rule—a reign of terror. Instead of living a life of faith with their hearts filled with hope, love, joy, and peace, fear would dominate. God warned, "In their homes terror will reign," and death would stalk their streets in many forms: a wasting famine, a deadly plague, wild beasts and poisonous snakes—and worst of all, cruel soldiers marching in their streets with sharp swords, sparing no one, young or old. Their enemies would slaughter and scatter the whole nation. Then the Lord would say to them:

> Where now are your gods?
> Let them rise up to help you!
> Let them give you shelter!

Moses' sad song was like the singing of a nightmare, with frightening images of the future—but thankfully the last words of the song conveyed hope: hope in God's Love, mercy, and compassion for his people, and hope in God's mighty power to punish his enemies and restore his people to life. In Moses' song the Lord said:

> "See now that I myself am He! There is no god besides me.
> I put to death and I bring to life,
> I have wounded and I will heal. . . .
> Rejoice, O nations, with his people,
> For he will avenge the blood of his servants;
> He will take vengeance on his enemies
> And make atonement for his land and his people.

And so the sad song of Moses came to an end with a great word of hope. God would make atonement for his land and his people. He would cover them with his Love, with his mercy, with his forgiveness. Imagine how it must have been that day when Moses first recited all the words of that sad song, and all Israel with one voice sang it after him. Sorrow must have enveloped all who heard those words testifying to God's goodness and faithfulness and their own wretchedness, wickedness, and faithlessness. O Israel, take to heart the words of that sad song. O Israel, hope in the Lord!

A Blessing

Thankfully, the words of that unhappy song were not Moses' last words to the Israelites. The final words that Moses, the man of God, pronounced on them before his death were words of blessing and of Love from the Lord. Moses reminded the people of God's great Love for them, and how God had come to them on Mount Horeb as Israel's great King when he gave Israel his holy law, shining forth over them with a burst of brilliance like the dawn of day. "Surely he loved the people!" declared Moses. Then Moses blessed Israel tribe by tribe.[8]

Reuben. Moses honoured the firstborn son of Jacob by blessing that tribe first. Moses blessed Reuben with life! "Let Reuben live and not die."

Judah. Next Moses blessed the fourth-born son of Jacob, honouring that tribe with the second blessing. Not only was Judah the largest and strongest tribe, it was also the tribe from which the Messiah would come. Moses said, "Hear, O Lord, the cry of Judah. . . . Be his help against his foes."

Levi. Moses blessed this tribe of priests, saying of Levi, "He watched over your word and guarded your covenant. He teaches . . . your law to Israel. He offers incense before you and whole burnt offerings on your altar. Bless all his skills, O Lord, and be pleased with the work of his hands."

Benjamin. Moses blessed this youngest son of Jacob with these words: "Let the beloved of the Lord rest secure in him, for he shields him all day long. Let the one the Lord loves rest between his shoulders."

Joseph. Jacob's favorite son received the most generous blessing from Moses— the finest and the choicest things that the land could yield. Moses said, "May the Lord bless his land . . . with the best gifts of the earth . . . and the favour of him who dwelt in the burning bush." There was no greater blessing than God's favour! Moses also blessed the two sons of Joseph—Ephraim and Manasseh—with the riches of the land and the successes of war, so that Ephraim and Manasseh would be both wealthy and mighty tribes.

Zebulun and Issachar. These two tribes would be side by side in the Promised Land, and Moses blessed them together. He told Zebulun and Issachar to rejoice because God would bless them. In their lands they would worship the Lord and "offer sacrifices of righteousness." Their lands were bounded by the Great Sea and the Sea of Galilee. Moses said, "They will feast on the abundance of the seas, on the treasures hidden in the sand."

Gad. Moses said, "Blessed is he who enlarges Gad's domain!" The tribe of Gad already had conquered its territory on the east side of the Jordan River. "He chose the best land for himself; the leader's portion was kept for him." Concerning that tribe Moses declared, "He carried out the Lord's righteous will."

Dan. Moses said, "Dan is a lion's cub, springing out of Bashan." Bashan was a mountain noted for fierce lions, who would descend the mountain to leap upon their prey in the plains.

Naphtali. Moses said, "Naphtali is abounding with the favour of the Lord and is full of his blessing." The Sea of Galilee was in Naphtali's territory. We read concerning that region, "The people living in darkness have seen a great light; on those living in the land of the shadow of death, a light has dawned."[9] That light was the light of the world, Jesus Christ, who lived and preached in Capernaum in the land of Naphtali.

Asher. Moses said, "Most blessed of sons is Asher."

Moses then praised the God of Israel, "who rides on the heavens to help you and on the clouds of his majesty." Moses urged the people to seek refuge in the eternal God and safety in his everlasting arms. There they would be secure. Moses then blessed the entire nation. "Blessed are you, O Israel! Who is like you, a people saved by the Lord? He is your shield and helper and your glorious sword!"[10]

LESSON 13: TEACHER'S GUIDE

A Book, a Song, and a Blessing

VISUAL AIDS:

Show your students a famous book, a famous song, and a famous blessing—the creative works of different people. But the works of Moses are unique in that they are also the prophetic words of God!

MEMORY WORK:

"All men are like grass, and all their glory is like the flowers of the field. The grass withers and the flowers fall, but the word of our God endures forever."

Isaiah 40:6, 8

"My thoughts are not your thoughts, neither are your ways my ways," declares the Lord. My word that goes out from my mouth will not return to me empty, but will accomplish what I desire and achieve the purpose for which I sent it."

Isaiah 55:8, 11

A NEW TESTAMENT BLESSING:

"Now may the Lord of Peace himself give you peace at all times and in every way. The grace of our Lord Jesus Christ be with you all."

2 Thessalonians 3:16, 18

REVIEW QUESTIONS:

1. What three things did Moses do to ensure that his words would endure after he died?
2. Why was it so important to Moses that his words be preserved for future generations?

3. What kind of song did Moses give to the Israelites to sing? What did this song say would happen in the future?
4. Why was this song a reliable prophecy? Why did Moses give Israel this song?
5. Moses' final words to the Israelites were not the woes of that unhappy song. What were the final words of Moses to Israel?

PRAYER:

O Lord, we thank you for giving us your words in so many ways—in the books and songs and blessings of the Bible. Amen.

PSALMS TO SING:

"The truth of the Lord endures forever" (Psalm 117).

117B . . . and 100AC; 111B; 146AB

These are just a few of the psalms urging us to sing songs to the Lord. "O sing a new song to the Lord. All earth sing to the Lord" (Psalm 96). "I'll sing to the Lord as long as I live; sing praise to my God while life he will give" (Psalm 104).

96A; 98AB; 118C (14, 17) . . . and 7B (9); 13 (5); 27E; 28A (1, 2, 6–8); 33A (1); 40ABE (1); 47A; 51E; 57B; 61; 66A (1–3, 7); 67A; 69E (20–22); 71D; 89A (1); 92A; 95A (1, 2); 100AB; 104E; 105A; 108A; 138AB (1); 145A; 147A (1); 149

In the book of Psalms, God pours out "showers of blessings" upon his people. "Blest they who in thy strength confide and in whose hearts are pilgrims' ways. They make the vale of tears a spring, with showers of blessings covering" (Psalm 84).

67AB . . . and 3 (5); 5AB (1, 5); 21A; 24AC (1–3); 29A (1, 6); 84A; 89D; 112A (1); 115BD; 116A; 118C; 128AB; 134AB; 146AB

Lesson 14

THE DEATH OF MOSES

- Deuteronomy 32:48–52; 34:1–12
- Psalm 90;
- Luke 9:28–36

On the same day that the Israelites sang Moses' sad song, and recited his blessings, the Lord said to Moses, "Go up . . . and view Canaan, the land I am giving the Israelites as their own possession. There on the mountain that you have climbed you will die and be gathered to your people."[1] The last thing Moses did before he climbed the mountain to die was to bless the Israelites tribe by tribe. He pronounced blessing after blessing upon them. To the very end of his life, Moses served the Lord by ministering to the people.

Moses' Ministry on Earth

Moses once wrote this prayer: "May the beauty of the Lord our God rest upon us; establish the work of our hands for us—yes, establish the work of our hands."[2] And God answered that prayer for Moses. Although he faced satanic assaults almost every day of his life, assailed on every side by the evil one, still God accomplished great things through him. The book of Deuteronomy ends with this eulogy: "No prophet has arisen in Israel like Moses, whom the Lord knew face to face, who did all those miraculous signs and wonders the Lord sent him to do in Egypt. . . . For no one has ever shown the mighty power or performed the awesome deeds that Moses did in the sight of all Israel."[3]

Moses ministered to his people until the end of his life. He delivered his people from slavery, and led them on a forty-year journey from the land of bondage to the edge of the Land of Promise. And he was the mediator of the old covenant between the Lord and his people, giving them God's law—the Ten Commandments.

But it was not only to his people—and not only during his lifetime—that Moses ministered. He gave God's law to the whole world as well. Moses wrote the Pentateuch, the first five books of the Bible, as well as Psalm 90—and those words have helped people for centuries. In those books, Moses prophesied about the coming of the prophet—pointing not to himself as saviour, but to the Messiah, proclaiming the gospel of Jesus Christ, the Son of God, long before Jesus was even born. Moses has been a great evangelist and best-selling author for four thousand years![4]

Satan's Attacks on Moses

Moses once wrote that the entire span of our years is but "trouble and sorrow" and that we "finish our years with a moan."[5] Indeed, throughout his life, he faced one assault after another from Satan, the one who seeks to destroy God's servants.[6] Moses' life was not an easy one, but God delivered him again and again. As a tiny newborn baby in Egypt, Moses, by the king's command, should have been drowned in the Nile like the other Hebrew boys—but God rescued the infant Moses, using first his real mother and then his adopted mother, an Egyptian princess, to protect and preserve his life. As he grew up in Pharaoh's court, Moses should have been ensnared by the pleasures and treasures of Egypt, but again God rescued him. "By faith, Moses left Egypt, not fearing the king's anger"[7]—and the Lord preserved his life and faith for many years in the land of Midian. When Moses returned to Egypt, he should have been destroyed by an angry Pharaoh and his mighty army, but again and again God protected Moses and eventually rescued the Israelites by Moses' hands. And for forty years in the wilderness, Moses faced the constant rebellion of the

Israelites, with his life often in danger from his own people, but God delivered Moses from every harm.

However, the war with Satan did not stop with the death of Moses. The devil would continue to assault the people of God as he tried to arrest the promises of God. Above all, Satan desired to stop God's Son from securing salvation for the world.

Before the Saviour suffered the crucifixion—the greatest battle of all—Moses was called down from heaven to meet with Jesus on a high mountain and to talk to Jesus about his death. In his mortal body, Moses' feet never touched the Promised Land; but in his resurrection body—which was immortal, spiritual, imperishable, and radiant with glorious splendour—Moses did stand on a mountaintop in the land of Israel. There he spoke to the one who was greater than himself, the one promised from the beginning, the one about whom Moses himself had prophesied—Jesus Christ our Lord, who offered himself as a sacrifice for many.

Moses' Final Ascent

Many times the Israelites had watched Moses climb a mountain to be with God, and always Moses had come back down to them. This time, Moses would not return. He would die on top of the mountain with God and be buried on top of the mountain by God. The Israelites would never see Moses again.[8]

And so Moses climbed Mount Nebo in the land of Moab to die. Although he was one hundred and twenty years old, his strength had not left him. On the last day of his long life, his legs were not too frail to climb a mountain, nor were his eyes too dim to view the landscape. There, on top of the mountain, the Lord showed Moses the whole Promised Land and said to him, "This is the land I promised on oath to Abraham, Isaac, and Jacob. . . . I have let you see it with your own eyes, but you will not cross over into it."[9]

There was something very sad about Moses' end on earth: Because of his sin, Moses never entered the Promised Land. He died and was buried in Moab. That same day God once again told him why he could not enter the Promised Land: "This is because you broke faith with me in the presence of the Israelites . . . and because you did not uphold my holiness among the Israelites. Therefore, you will see the land only from a distance. You will not enter the land I am giving to the people of Israel."[10] The bones of Joseph would be carried across the Jordan River and they would be buried in the Promised Land, but the bones of Moses would remain in an unmarked grave in the land of Moab forever. God keeps his promises—all of them.

In spite of this deep disappointment, it must have been wonderful for Moses, on the last day of his life, to finally see the land promised by God. For four hundred years the Israelites had been waiting for that land; for forty years Moses had been leading them to that land—and now there it was before him. What a beautiful sight it must have been—that good, green land stretching beyond the sparkle of the Jordan River, all the way to the Mediterranean Sea shimmering on the horizon.

Moses could also see the tents of the Israelites camped below him on the plain, as numerous as the sand on a seashore. God had brought them here, just as he had promised. And the Lord, because of his great Love, had used Moses to bring it all to pass. On his last day in this world, Moses could see his life's work before him—the work of bringing the Israelites from Egypt to Canaan. What a joy it must have been for Moses to stand upon that mountain and see with his own eyes what God had accomplished through him—and what he had accomplished through God!

Entering into God's Rest

How long Moses gazed at the Promised Land from that mountaintop we do not know. Perhaps as he looked westward, God allowed him to see one final glorious sunset on earth before he saw the surpassing glory of the Lord in heaven. Perhaps Moses was allowed one last time to see the moon and stars twinkling and shining over the Holy Land. But every day and every life comes to an end. Moses, the servant of the Lord, died on top of the mountain. He was not alone, for the Lord was with him there, talking to him, as a man talks to his friend. Moses spent his last moments on earth just as he had spent most of his life: in the blessed presence of his God.

Moses once prayed, "Relent, O Lord! How long will it be? Have compassion on your servants. Satisfy us in the morning with your unfailing Love, that we may sing for joy and be glad all our days. Make us glad for as many days as you have afflicted us, for as many years as we have seen trouble."[11] At last, that prayer of Moses was answered. God granted him an eternity of rest and peace and joy—in heaven.

Moses' final resting place was on top of a mountain overlooking the Land of Promise. When he died, God himself buried the body of Moses, and angels attended his funeral—but no fellow human being came to weep by his graveside, for no one knew where Moses was buried. God left no tombstone to visit or relic to worship, lest the remains of Moses became a snare to the people. The body of Moses was laid to rest where dust would return to dust with no one to disturb it.

God's Faithful Servant

Moses persevered in his faith to the end of his life. When the time had come for his departure, Moses could say, "I have fought the good fight; I have finished the race; I have kept the faith. Now there is in store for me the crown of righteousness, which the Lord, the righteous Judge, will award to me on that day—and not only to me, but also to all who have longed for his appearing."[12] The book of Hebrews tells us that "Moses was faithful as a servant in all God's house," doing what God required of him,[13] speaking what God revealed to him. When Moses died and went to be with the Lord, surely he would hear these words from his master: "Well done, my good and faithful servant!" There can be no greater establishment or acknowledgement of our work on earth than hearing those words spoken to us by our Lord.

LESSON 14: TEACHER'S GUIDE

The Death of Moses

VISUAL AIDS:

Panoramic views of the Holy Land—what Moses might have seen from the mountain—would be useful for this lesson. Also, cut out obituaries or photos of funerals from a newspaper, to show what people do to mourn the death of loved ones.

MEMORY WORK:

> "O Lord, . . . satisfy us in the morning with your unfailing Love, that we may sing for joy and be glad all our days."
>
> Psalm 90:14

> "May the favour of the Lord our God rest upon us. Establish the work of our hands for us; yes, establish the work of our hands."
>
> Psalm 90:17

REVIEW QUESTIONS:

1. What did Moses give the Israelites before he climbed the mountain to die?
2. What did Moses see from the top of Mount Nebo in Moab?
3. Who wept for Moses after he died? Who buried the body of Moses, and where was his grave?
4. Whose bones were carried into the Promised Land? Whose bones were not carried into the Promised Land?
5. What were some of the major battles in Moses' life?

6. After Moses' body had been dead and buried for two thousand years, God sent Moses from heaven to the land of Israel. What was Moses sent to do?
7. What were some of the great works that God accomplished through Moses and that Moses accomplished through God?

PRAYER:

O Lord, we also pray as Moses prayed: Establish the work of our hands. May the things we do in this life be pleasing in your sight, O God, and may we have joy in our work, knowing that our labours in the Lord are not in vain. O Lord, thank you for your Word and your Love which strengthens us, and for Jesus Christ, through whom we can do all things. May each one of us live a life of faith, day by day, until the day we die. Amen.

PSALM TO SING:

Psalm 90—the prayer of Moses, the man of God!

Lesson 15

ONE GREATER THAN MOSES

• Hebrews 3:1–6

Moses was a great man of God, declared to be "faithful as a servant in all God's house," but "Christ is faithful as a son over God's house." Moses was an honoured servant of God, but Hebrews tells us, "Jesus has been found worthy of greater honour than Moses."[1] For God's law was given through Moses, but grace and truth came through Jesus Christ.[2]

The One with an Indestructible Life

God is eternal, but man is mortal.[3] Even though Moses was the greatest Old Testament prophet, he died and was buried, and over the centuries even his bones vanished, disintegrating into dust. As God declared when man first sinned, "Dust you are and to dust you will return."[4] Moses wrote, "You turn men back to dust, saying, 'Return to dust, O sons of men.' All our days pass away. . . . They quickly pass, and we fly away."[5] Moses lived one hundred and twenty years, but his life quickly passed from this earth, taking up only a small portion of eternity.

But there came into the world a man who was greater than the prophet Moses, because he was a man who conquered death: the man Jesus. Jesus' years on earth were far fewer than Moses' years—in fact, Moses lived on earth almost four times as long as Jesus did. However, when our Saviour was killed in the prime of his life, the grave could not hold him, though he was crucified on a cross, and died, and was buried in a tomb! His body did not decay, nor did his bones turn to dust. All this was prophesied about him hundreds of years before he was born: "I am laid in the dust of death. A band of evil men has encircled me; they have pierced my hands and my feet. Keep me safe, O God, for in you I take refuge. My body will rest secure, because you will not abandon me to the grave, nor will you let your Holy One see decay."[6]

Jesus was laid in a tomb, but on the third day he rose from the dead to declare: "Do not be afraid! I am the First and the Last. I am the Living One. I was dead, and behold, I am alive for ever and ever! And I hold the keys of death and hell."[7] Jesus Christ our Lord is greater than Moses—he is the one who conquered death, the one who was "declared with power to be the Son of God by his resurrection from the dead," the one who became a priest forever "on the basis of the power of an indestructible life."[8]

The One Without Sin

Not only did Jesus conquer death; he conquered sin. The sin which so easily entangles each one of us—which ensnared even Moses—did not trip or trap or even touch Christ. He was not deceived or enticed by the temptations that Satan hurled at him. He alone in the history of the human race was able to stay faithful to God and stand firm against the onslaught of fiery arrows aimed at his heart by the evil one. Even Moses, the faithful servant of God, fell into grievous sins: breaking faith with God, not trusting God, and not honouring God as holy in the sight of Israel.[9]

But even as Christ hung on the cross, he trusted God before all the people gathered there to watch him die, and he prayed this psalm from his broken heart: "My God, my God, why have you forsaken me? Why are you so far from saving me, so far from the words of my groaning? O my God, I cry out by day, but you do not answer, by night, and am not silent. Yet you are enthroned as the Holy One; you are the praise of Israel."[10] Even as he hung on the cross dying, Jesus trusted in God and honoured him as holy before all Israel. As he died on the cross, Jesus called out with a loud voice for all to hear, "Father, into your hands I commit my spirit."[11] With his dying breath he trusted God. He had not ceased—not once—to trust in God, from the time he took his first breath as a newborn baby until he breathed his last upon the cross. Jesus alone lived his whole life by faith—perfectly.

The One Who Performed Miracles of Grace

We read in the Old Testament that no other prophet arose in Israel like Moses, "Who did all those miraculous signs and wonders the Lord sent him to do in Egypt. . . . No one has ever shown the mighty power or performed the awesome deeds that Moses did in the sight of all Israel."[12] While Moses performed mighty miracles, most of them were dread-filled acts of death and destruction. Jesus also performed mighty miracles, but—with the exception of the drowning of some pigs and the withering of the fig tree—they were miracles of life and grace.

Jesus brought healing and blessing, as the prophecies promised. To prove that he was the Messiah, the prophet promised by Moses, Jesus said, "The blind receive sight; the lame walk; those who have leprosy are cured, the deaf hear, the dead are raised, and the good news is preached to the poor. Blessed is the man who does not fall away on account of me."[13]

Moses was the greatest prophet in Israel until the one he had prophesied about came. Moses brought the light of the God's law and of God's Word, but Jesus brought the words of eternal life! "In him was life and that life was the light of men."[14] Moses was the mediator of the old covenant between God and Israel, but Jesus Christ was the mediator of the new covenant by which men might be saved from sin and death. Ultimately, there could only be one perfect mediator between God and man, between heaven and earth—and that mediator was from both heaven and earth; he was both man and God—he was Jesus Christ our Lord.

LESSON 15: TEACHER'S GUIDE

One Greater Than Moses

VISUAL AIDS:

For this lesson you will need pictures associated with death: cemeteries, funerals, coffins, skulls and skeletons, etc. Jesus—the one greater than Moses—came into the world and conquered both sin and death.

MEMORY WORK:

"The wages of sin is death, but the gift of God is eternal life in Christ Jesus our Lord."

Romans 6:23

"Because of his great Love for us, God, who is rich in mercy, made us alive with Christ even when we were dead in sins. It is by grace you have been saved."

Ephesians 2:4–5

"Death has been swallowed up in victory. The sting of death is sin, and the power of sin is the law. But thanks be to God! He gives us the victory through our Lord Jesus Christ."

1 Corinthians 15:54, 56–57

REVIEW QUESTIONS:

1. How was Jesus' life different than Moses'? How were their deaths different?
2. How did sin affect Moses? How did it affect Jesus?
3. How were Jesus' miracles different than Moses'? What does this tell us about Jesus?

PRAYER:

O Lord, we thank you for the work of Jesus Christ, who brought us near to you. His death bought us peace with you. We thank you for his great victory over sin and death. We thank you that he came to destroy the works of the devil, and that in him we have forgiveness of sins and everlasting life. O Lord, we thank you for sending your Son, Jesus.

PSALMS TO SING:

16B, 118C. These are prophetic psalms declaring that God will not abandon his Holy One the grave, nor will he allow him to undergo decay.

Lesson 16

A NEW AND LIVING WAY

ANOTHER COVENANT, ANOTHER RIGHTEOUSNESS, ANOTHER CREATION

• Hebrews 8:6–13

The Revelation of a New Covenant

God repeatedly declared to Israel through Moses the secret of success: they must obey his covenant, the Ten Commandments. But God knew that Israel would fail to remain faithful to him. God said, "They will forsake me and break the covenant I made with them. They will turn to other gods and worship them, rejecting me and breaking my covenant."[1] From the beginning—from before the foundation of the world—God had a greater, more gracious, and supremely more glorious covenant planned for his people. This covenant would unite God and his people in an unbreakable relationship of Love forever.

When Moses again proclaimed the Ten Commandments and all the rest of God's law to the people in Deuteronomy, the old covenant was re-established. That the commandments were recorded a second time in Scripture emphasises their extreme and everlasting importance.[2] Nevertheless, the old covenant was a temporary covenant, one which God designed to be replaced. "If there had been nothing wrong with that first covenant, no place would have been sought for another one"—but God found fault with his people under that first covenant and declared that a new covenant was necessary. Scripture says, "By calling this covenant 'new,' he has made the first one obsolete"—an old covenant which soon would disappear.[3] How could that be? God's holy law is eternal—established to last forever!

The problem was with the people, not with God's law, for "the law of the Lord is perfect."[4] Even the new covenant affirms that "the law is holy and the commandment is holy, righteous and good."[5] No fault could be found with those laws; the fault was with the people. This was what the Sovereign Lord said to Israel in her unfaithfulness: "I will deal with you as you deserve, because you have despised my oath by breaking the covenant."[6] They were the ones who must change—but they could not effect this change themselves. God was the one who would make a new covenant with them, delivering them from the rule of sin and the curse of the law by which they were still held captive. "I will remember the covenant I made with you in the days of your youth [the old covenant] and I will establish an everlasting covenant with you [the new covenant]. Then you will remember your ways and be ashamed. . . . So I will establish my covenant with you and you will know that I am the Lord."[7]

God's Promise Through His Prophets (Jeremiah 31:31–34)

This is what God says: "I am the Lord; that is my name! I will not give my glory to another or my praise to idols. See, the former things have taken place, and new things I declare. Before they spring into being, I announce them to you."[8] What were these "new things" that God announced to Israel long before they happened? God declared the advent of his servant, the promised Messiah, through whom God would fulfil all his promises of Love by establishing an everlasting covenant of peace between himself and his people.[9]

When the Messiah came to Israel to make atonement for all their sins, God promised through the prophet Ezekiel that his servant would reign over them. "My servant will be their prince forever."[10] Zechariah also proclaimed the coming of Christ—the King of the Jews, the King of the world—"Rejoice greatly, O Daughter of Zion! Shout, Daughter of Jerusalem! See, your king comes to you, righteous and having salvation, gentle and riding on a donkey. . . . He will proclaim peace to the nations. His rule will extend from sea to sea . . . to the ends of the earth."[11]

Jesus Christ was God's promised servant who became our prince of peace. He purchased our peace with God through his suffering and death upon the cross. So it was prophesied: "The punishment that brought us peace was upon him."[12] God promised, "[My people] will no longer defile themselves with their idols and vile images or with any of their offenses, for I will save them from all their sinful backsliding, and I will cleanse them. They will be my people, and I will be their God. . . . They will follow my laws and be careful to keep my decrees. I will make a covenant of peace with them; it will be an everlasting covenant."[13]

Jesus Christ himself was that servant who, by the sacrifice of himself, would free us from the prison of our own dark souls.[14] His life's blood, poured out for the cleansing of our sins, was the guarantee of the new and eternal covenant which would secure for us peace with God and everlasting life—the new covenant through which the prisoners of sin and death would be set free forever from the terrifying abyss of outer darkness and eternal death.[15]

Malachi, another prophet of God, referred to the Messiah as the "messenger of the covenant." Through Malachi God announced, "Suddenly, the Lord you are seeking will come to his temple; the messenger of the covenant whom you desire, will come."[16] The one for whom they were watching and waiting was Jesus—the mediator and messenger of the new covenant. "For there is one God and one mediator between God and men—the man Christ Jesus, who gave himself as a ransom for all men. . . . Christ is the mediator of a new covenant, that those who are called may receive the promised eternal inheritance—now that he has died as a ransom to set them free from the sins committed under the first covenant."[17]

Even in the old covenant, God was calling his people to the eternal life of the new covenant: "Give ear and come to me! Hear me that your soul may live! I will make an everlasting covenant with you. . . . Seek the Lord while he may be found; call on him while he is near. Let the wicked forsake his way and the evil man his thoughts. Let him turn to the Lord, and he will have mercy on him; let him turn to our God, for he will freely pardon."[18]

Through the many prophets he sent to Israel, the Lord clearly proclaimed his desire for a new covenant. In this new covenant, God would not write his law in letters upon tablets of stone, as he did in the old covenant, but he would write it on human hearts by his Spirit. This new covenant would not be "of the letter, but of the Spirit, for the letter [of the law] kills, but the Spirit [of the Lord] gives life."[19] How great and glorious was that new covenant which God would make with his people! God's law would be written in their minds, and God's Love would be poured out in their hearts by the power of God's Holy Spirit working within them. Rejoice, for Jesus has become the mediator of another, better covenant—the new covenant!

The Revelation of a New Righteousness (Romans 3:21–31)

The Lord said to the Israelites, "You must obey my laws and be careful to follow my decrees. I am the Lord your God."[20] But woe to Israel and to the entire human race, if this was our only hope for life! We all together would fail and perish because "justice is far from us and righteousness does not reach us. . . . For our offenses are many in [God's] sight, and our sins testify against us."[21] God's holy law is the standard, showing us who we must be and how we must live to be righteous in the sight of God—and we all fail to attain that standard of perfection. God's Word states, "No one will be declared righteous in his sight by observing the law."[22]

Moses spoke of the righteousness that is by law through keeping God's commandments, saying, "The man who obeys them will live by them."[23] That was true—but who could obey them perfectly? Jesus was the only man who fulfilled all the requirements of God's holy law, living a sinless life in perfect obedience to the commandments of God.[24]

If we could attain righteousness—if reconciliation to God were possible through our own efforts—then Christ pouring out his soul unto death was a pointless and useless sacrifice that benefited no one. "If righteousness could be attained through the law, then Christ died for nothing."[25] But Christ died because it was the only way that we might have life. "At just the right time, when we were still powerless, Christ died for the ungodly. . . . God demonstrates his own Love for us in this: While we were still sinners, Christ died for us. When we were God's enemies, we were reconciled to him through the death of his Son."[26] How could we, through our own efforts, be reconciled to God "when we were dead," "when we were still powerless," "while we were still sinners," "when we were God's enemies?"

There was nothing we could do to bring us peace with God, but, "since we have been justified by faith, we have peace with God through our Lord Jesus Christ . . . through whom we have now received reconciliation."[27] We have hope, for "now a righteousness from God, apart from the law, has been made known. . . . This righteousness from God comes through faith in Jesus Christ to all who believe."[28] We cannot justify ourselves. God is the one who justifies those who have faith in Jesus. The new covenant proclaims: "A man is justified by faith apart from observing the law!"[29] The gospel of Christ is "the power of God for the salvation of everyone who believes. . . . For in the gospel a righteousness from God is revealed, a righteousness that is by faith from first to last."[30]

Israel's Failure to Attain Righteousness Through the Law

It would be a deadly mistake to think that we can make ourselves righteous by keeping God's law. At times in Israel's history they pursued a righteousness by law, attempting to perform all the most minute requirements of the law, but they did not attain righteousness in this way. Was this not commendable? Why did they not attain righteousness?

The first and foremost reason is that they were not living by faith. They were trusting in themselves and in their own works to make themselves righteous, rather than trusting in God and in his powerful and merciful grace to cleanse their sins and transform their hearts. Israel, who pursued a law of righteousness, did not attain it, "because they pursued it not by faith but as if it were by works. . . . Since they did not know the righteousness that comes from God and sought to establish their own, they did not submit to God's righteousness."[31]

The second reason Israel did not attain righteousness is connected to the first. Their attention was so focused upon the many tiny requirements of the law that their mind became entangled in its details, and they missed the weightier matters of justice and mercy. They even missed the Messiah! God's law was always meant to point them to Christ and to his great salvation, but Israel thought it was a handbook on how to save themselves.

Their heads were buried in their law books and they did not recognize their Saviour even when he was standing in their midst.

Yes, Israel allowed the law to blind them to God's gift of grace; however, an equally fatal mistake would be forgetting and forsaking the law of God—that law which is "holy, righteous and good."[32] To neglect or despise God's law would lead only to death. "Be sure of this: the wicked will not go unpunished. . . . The wages of sin is death."[33] We are made righteous by the mercy of God, and saved by grace through faith, but that does not mean that we can neglect or despise God's law. God commands us to keep his law, even as Christ Jesus left us an example of perfection for us to follow. Christ did not abolish God's law; he fulfilled it and confirmed it.

Righteousness by Faith Promised from the Beginning

Righteousness by faith was not a doctrine introduced for the first time in the new covenant; it was also proclaimed in the old covenant. "Now a righteousness from God apart from law has been made known, "to *which the law and the prophets testify!*"[34]

Moses understood and testified that there are two kinds of righteousness: the righteousness that is by law and the righteousness that is by faith.[35] Moses was the mediator of the old covenant, the prophet who gave God's law to Israel and continually exhorted them to obey that law, the man who carried in his own arms the stone tablets with the Ten Commandments, the author who wrote in every one of his books about the necessity of keeping God's commands—and yet even he knew that there was another righteousness, a righteousness apart from the law. The other Old Testament prophets also understood this. "The just shall live by faith!" That triumphant truth was proclaimed in the old covenant—a cry of victory for the whole human race—we who were trapped in sin, unable to free ourselves from the power of Satan.[36]

In his first book of the law Moses proclaimed loudly and clearly that God credits faith as righteousness.[37] Moses wrote about Abraham, the father of faith, testifying that "Abraham believed God and it was credited to him as righteousness."[38] It was Abraham's faith, not his works, that God counted as righteous. "Against all hope, Abraham in hope believed. . . . He did not waver through unbelief regarding the promise of God, but was strengthened in his faith and gave glory to God, being fully persuaded that

God had power to do what he had promised. That is why 'it was credited to him as righteousness.'" Those words "were not written for him alone, but also for us, to whom God will credit righteousness—for us who believe in him who raised Jesus our Lord from the dead."[39]

Most impressively, Moses knew deep within his own heart and from his own life that there was a righteousness apart from the law, a righteousness that was by faith. Moses' hope for justification was not in his own works, for he knew that he had fallen far short of perfection. Because of his sins Moses was not allowed to enter the Promised Land on earth,[40] but God permitted him to enter the paradise of heaven—because a person is justified by his faith, not by his works, and made righteous not by keeping the law, but by believing in God. Even Moses, God's faithful servant, was not perfectly faithful. He too had to rely on God's Love and mercy and forgiveness. Blessed is the one "to whom God credits righteousness apart from works."[41]

The Revelation of a New Creation

We read God's command in the old covenant Scriptures: "Repent! Turn away from all your offenses; then sin will not be your downfall. Rid yourselves of all your offenses you have committed, and get a new heart and a new spirit."[42] Nothing less than a complete transformation—in fact, a new creation—was necessary.

Where in the world would God's people find new hearts and spirits? How could they possibly obey this command? God answered these questions by declaring, "I will sprinkle clean water on you, and you will be clean. I will cleanse you. . . . I will give you a new heart and I will put a new spirit in you. I will remove from you your heart of stone and I will give you a heart of flesh. And I will put my Spirit in you and move you to follow my decrees and be careful to keep my laws. . . . I will save you from all your uncleanness."[43] God himself would work this great transformation within us. He would create in us new hearts by sending his Holy Spirit to dwell within us.[44] The new covenant Scriptures testify, "If anyone is in Christ, he is a new creation. The old has gone; the new has come! All this is from God, who reconciled us to himself through Christ."[45] When we believe in Christ and are united to Christ, we become new creatures.

But how can that be true? The new creature looks exactly like the old creature, and the new person's voice is exactly like the old person's voice. No one would have any trouble identifying us by sight, sound, fingerprints, or DNA. Our bodies continue to function in exactly the same way: we do not suddenly sprout wings and fly; halos do not fall from heaven to crown the newest saints on earth; we do not start to glow or walk on water or glide through walls. No, it seems that we lead ordinary lives in ordinary bodies that get sick and weak and eventually die—just like the rest of the human race. So how are we new creatures in Christ?

We are different not in what is seen, but rather in what is hidden in our hearts and spirits. We have been made new by God, just as he promised: "I will give you a new heart and I will put a new spirit in you."[46] Although our bodies stay the same, our hearts and spirits are made new in Christ. He shines his light in us and fills us with himself.[47] This is a great mystery and a great reality: "Christ in you, the hope of glory!"[48]

A heart changed by God is a heart full of faith, joy, and peace—overflowing with hope by the power of the Holy Spirit and with thankfulness to the Lord; a heart full of love, for "God has poured out his Love into our hearts by the Holy Spirit whom he has given us."[49] Sadly, having an empty heart and being alienated from God is the reality of unbelievers' lives. "The fool says in his heart, 'There is no God.'"[50] In the Bible, a fool means "an empty person," a person who does not believe in God and whose heart is void of faith, hope, or love. That person is "separate from Christ . . . without hope and without God in the world."[51] In fact, there is an evil spirit at work in the hearts of all who are disobedient to God,[52] but "we have not received the spirit of the world but the Spirit who is from God."[53]

Because we have received the promised Holy Spirit by faith, our hearts and our minds are transformed. We have "the mind of Christ," and are being "transformed into his likeness with ever-increasing glory, which comes from the Lord, who is the Spirit."[54] And our poor earthly bodies, by God's amazing grace, become the temple of the Holy Spirit of God![55] Now God commands us to live in accordance with our new, transformed selves. Our lives must be ruled by the Spirit of God who dwells in us. Those who are in Christ Jesus "do not live according to the sinful nature, but according to the Spirit. Those controlled by the sinful nature cannot please God. You, however, are controlled not by the sinful nature, but by the Spirit, if the Spirit of God lives in you."[56]

By God's grace, he has given each of us a new heart, a new mind, a new nature, a new spirit. God has kept his promises. He has created in us a new heart; he has imparted to us a new spirit, the Holy Spirit of God himself. Jesus Christ came to release us from the power of Satan and the power of our own sinful nature, by putting in us a new spirit, the Holy Spirit of God himself. Christ dwelling in our hearts through his Holy Spirit—this is the miraculous transformation of our hearts. God has changed us; we are new creatures in Christ!

LESSON 16: TEACHER'S GUIDE

A New and Living Way

VISUAL AIDS:

There are examples in nature of complete transformation or metamorphosis[56]—such as a caterpillar changing into a butterfly. You can bring pictures of the four stages of a monarch butterfly (egg, larva, pupa and adult insect).

An even better visual aid would be to catch a monarch caterpillar (which you can find on a milkweed plant in late summer) and watch its real-life transformation. Feed the caterpillar plenty of milkweed leaves. When it is large enough, it will form a beautiful bright green chrysalis with a shiny gold "zipper." The chrysalis will then turn black and eventually hatch into a gorgeous butterfly. This is a very easy project. I have hatched hundreds of these butterflies with my own children!

MEMORY WORK:

Jesus said, "This is my blood of the covenant, which is poured out for many for the forgiveness of sins."

Matthew 26:28

"Christ is the mediator of a new covenant."

Hebrews 9:15

"In the gospel a righteousness from God is revealed, a righteousness that is by faith from first to last."

Romans 1:17

"Now a righteousness from God apart from the law has been made known, to which the law and the prophets testify. This righteousness from God comes through faith in Jesus Christ to all who believe."

Romans 3:21–22

> "If anyone is in Christ, he is a new creature. The old has gone; the new has come! All this is from God, who reconciled us to himself through Christ."
>
> 2 Corinthians 5:17–18

REVIEW QUESTIONS:

The Revelation of a New Covenant

1. The old covenant was a temporary covenant, one which God designed to be replaced. Why was a new covenant necessary? What was wrong with the old covenant?
2. How did God inform the people of his plans for a new covenant?
3. Was God's law abandoned in the new covenant? What does the new covenant affirm about God's law?
4. The law of God was written in letters on tablets of stone in the old covenant and then placed in the Holy of Holies in the tabernacle and the temple. Where did God say he would write his holy law in the new covenant? How would God do this?
5. Why is the new covenant called the covenant of peace? Who is called the prince of peace, and the messenger of the covenant? Why?

Although both covenants came from God and came with glory, there are many contrasts between them. You could make a fill-in-the-blank page of opposites as a different kind of test for your students.

a) The old covenant was replaced by the new covenant.

b) The former covenant was temporary; the latter covenant was everlasting.

c) The letter of the law brings death; but the Spirit of the Lord gives life.

d) In the old covenant we are under law; in the new covenant we are under grace (Romans 6:14).

e) The wages of sin is death, but the gift of God is eternal life in Jesus Christ our Lord (Romans 6:23).

f) Count yourselves dead to sin, but alive to God (Romans 6:11).

g) Do not offer the parts of your body to sin as instruments of wickedness, but rather offer yourselves to God, and offer the parts of your body to him as instruments of righteousness (Romans 6:13).

The Revelation of a New Righteousness

1. Is it possible for us to be righteous in God's sight by keeping his holy law? Can anyone boast that they have accomplished their salvation by their own will or work, even by their best desires or efforts?
2. Has there lived any human being who was righteous in the sight of God according to the law? Who was it?
3. Since humans beings are sinful from birth and since it is impossible for us to lead a perfectly righteous life, how then are we saved?
4. What do the Scriptures teach about our spiritual condition before our salvation?
5. People fall into two fatal errors in dealing with God's law. What are these deadly mistakes?
6. Moses stressed the importance of keeping God's law, but he also understood the gospel—that a person is saved by God's grace, through faith. How did Moses point us to the gospel?

The Revelation of a New Creation

1. God commanded the people to get a new heart and a new spirit. How could they possibly do this?
2. Who did God promise to send to change us?
3. How can we be a new creation? What change must happen in our hearts?
4. Describe the human heart before and after being united with Christ.
5. The Bible speaks about our "old self" and our "new self." What do these terms mean? What does God command us to do with these two parts of our selves?
6. What does it mean for your body to be "a temple of the Holy Spirit?"

PRAYER:

O Lord, we thank you for your many gracious promises to us. We thank you for the new covenant and for providing a new and living way to bring us into fellowship with you. Not only did you send your Son to save us from our sins; you sent your Holy Spirit into our hearts to change us from the inside out. O God, it is such a privilege that you have bestowed upon us that our poor bodies should be the dwelling place of your mighty Spirit. Help us to live day by day, moment by moment, according to your Spirit working within us. Let us never quench your Spirit, but instead let us continually put to death our old selves. Lord, we thank you for the power you have given us to live a godly life by your Spirit.

PSALMS TO SING:

These psalms are prayers to God to renew our hearts and lives, pleading for him to restore us and revive us:

51BE . . . and 19BD; 23ABCD; 73C; 80A (1, 2, 6); 85A; 126A; 138AB

Lesson 17

THE GLORIOUS FREEDOM OF THE CHILDREN OF GOD

• Romans 6–8

The Old Testament records how the Israelites were enslaved by the Egyptians, who "made their lives bitter with hard labour," "worked them ruthlessly," and treated them brutally.[1] The Israelites were trapped in this evil empire, where their lives were filled with toil, pain, fear, and death. They knew only trouble and torment, and they were unable to escape. During that long time of cruel bondage, "the Israelites groaned in their slavery and cried out, and their cry for help . . . went up to God."[2]

Their cry went up to God—and he heard. The Lord said to Moses, "I have indeed seen the misery of my people in Egypt. I have heard them crying out because of their slave drivers, and I am concerned about their suffering. So I have come down to rescue them. So now, go. I am sending you to Pharaoh to bring my people the Israelites out of Egypt."[3] The Israelites had been forced into slavery to serve a wicked ruler and build his evil empire, but the Lord sent Moses to set them free to serve the living God.

The New Testament records the work and the words of the one greater than Moses, who was also sent by God to lead his people out of bondage into freedom—"the glorious freedom of the children of God."[4] Who are the children of God? The Bible states, "To all who received [Jesus Christ], to those who believed in his name, he gave the right to become children of God," and, "You are all sons of God through faith in Jesus Christ."[5]

There is a glorious freedom for the children of God. Jesus himself said: "If the Son sets you free, you will be free indeed."[6] Jesus frees us from the power of sin, from the condemnation of the law, and from the hopelessness of the grave.

Freedom from Sin

"You know that [Christ] appeared so that he might take away our sins. The reason the Son of God appeared was to destroy the devil's work. The blood of Jesus . . . purifies us from all sin."[7] Not only are we released from the guilt of the sins we have committed and the punishment that those sins deserved—our union with Christ by faith actually frees us from the power of sin that works destruction within us.

When we were separate from Christ, sin ran rampant in our lives. It was the ruling force controlling our lives and we were powerless to stop it—even though we may have tried to do so in our own strength. Jesus declared, "I tell you the truth, everyone who sins is a slave to sin"[8]—and we all fall into that category.[9] God's Word states again and again that we are slaves of sin, ruled by sin, bound by sin.[10] Sin reigned in our mortal bodies so that we obeyed its evil desires. Sin was our master. Each one of us was "sold as a slave to sin" and "a prisoner to the law of sin" at work within the members of our bodies.[11] "All of us lived . . . at one time gratifying the cravings of our sinful nature and following its desires and thoughts. At that time we were separate from Christ . . . without hope and without God in the world."[12] How bleak was our bondage to sin! How sad was the state of our enslaved souls!

But "when we were still powerless; . . . while we were still sinners, Christ died for us. When we were God's enemies, we were reconciled to him through the death of his Son."[13] The death of Jesus Christ was the single most important event in all of human history, because it freed the world from the strangle-hold that sin had on every person's soul. Christ's death was the only act powerful enough to stop the virulent spread of sin within each human heart, and to counteract the potency of the evil ravaging this world. Even a cataclysmic occurrence such as the worldwide flood in Noah's time could not wash away the world's sin. Behold the Lamb of God, who alone can take away the sin of the world!

The Son of God, our Saviour, conquered sin in our lives through his death on the cross, and our union with Christ also means that "we have been united with him in his death. For we know that our old [sin-controlled] self was crucified with him, so that the body of sin might be rendered powerless, that we should no longer be slaves to sin—because anyone who has died has been freed from sin."[14] We died to sin! That is our great cry of victory in Christ. Sin can no longer deceive me or destroy me, driving me to eternal death—I have already died.[15]

It is good that we died, for we were evil creatures, controlled by sin and Satan, and trapped in the darkness of our own wickedness. Our old sinful selves were crucified with Christ so that, "just as Christ was raised from the dead . . . we too may live a new life. If we have been united with him like this in his death, we will certainly also be united with him in his resurrection."[16] By believing in Jesus and dying with him, we enter that glorious freedom of the children of God. Therein begins a transformation of our new selves into the likeness of Christ from glory to ever-increasing glory. "If anyone is in Christ, he is a new creation. The old has gone; the new has come."[17]

When our old sin-filled, sin-led, sin-ruled selves were put to death with Christ, we were set free to be born again by the Holy Spirit of God, to be filled with the Spirit and led by the Spirit. By God's grace we are no longer separate from Christ and alienated from God; instead, we are united to Christ and reconciled to God—and his indwelling Holy Spirit has become the controlling power working within us. It is no longer sin ruling our lives, but Christ, through his Holy Spirit in us.

Jesus Christ has set us free from sin! He set us free simply so that we would be free.[18] This is the amazing Love of God. He calls us to be free, living lives filled with love, peace, and joy. But we must not use that freedom to indulge the sinful nature.[19] Because we have been released—set free—from the power of sin, we should use that freedom to serve the one who saved us.

"To him who loves us and has freed us from our sins by his blood . . . be glory and power forever and ever!"[20]

Freedom from the Law

God's law was eternal, good, and holy—but not even Moses himself could keep the righteous requirements of the law, which he himself gave to Israel. The man who spoke face to face with God, and carried the Ten Commandments down the mountain in his own arms, was condemned by the words of the law which he instituted in Israel. Moses wrote, "you shall love the Lord your God with all your heart"[21]—the most important commandment of them all—but Moses himself failed in keeping that law; he could not enter the Promised Land because he failed to love, obey, and honour God.

But our Saviour fulfilled all the righteous requirements of God's law perfectly. Not only did Jesus keep the Ten Commandments, but he kept all the other laws of God completely, even the ceremonial laws. Jesus said it was proper for him to do this "to fulfil all righteousness."[22] He kept not only the letter of the law, but more importantly, he kept the spirit of the law. Jesus was the one man who did love God with all his heart, and he obeyed and honoured God unto death, even the humiliating and excruciating death upon the cross. He did not love his own life more than he loved God.

Jesus said, "Do not think I have come to abolish the law or the prophets; I have not come to abolish them but to fulfil them. I tell you the truth, until heaven and earth disappear, not the smallest letter, not the least stroke of the pen, will by any means disappear from the law until everything is accomplished."[23]

From beginning to end, the Scriptures declare that God established his holy law to last forever. If Jesus himself declared that God's law remains perfectly intact and totally in effect until the end of the world, how can we say that Jesus sets us free from the law? How can we read in the Bible that "we have been released from the law," and that in Christ we are no longer "under law?"[24]

First of all, Christ fulfilled the ceremonial laws of the Old Testament. These ceremonial laws "are a shadow of the things that were to come; the reality, however, is found in Christ."[25] We are released from the burden of keeping all these laws because they were simply shadows, pointing to Christ. For example, why would we now sacrifice a lamb for our sins when the Lamb of God himself has been sacrificed once for all to pay for sins? He was the lamb slain before the foundation of the world, and the entire sacrificial system of the Old Testament was merely a shadow of that eternal reality.

More importantly, Christ also fulfilled the moral laws of the Old Testament. If we are united to Christ by faith—if we are found in him and he is found in us—we who deserve condemnation are judged "not guilty." This is not because we have not sinned and broken God's law, but because if we are united to Christ, his perfect righteousness belongs to us and is imputed to us. Christ kept God's law perfectly for us all. If we are united to Christ, he has taken our sins upon himself and paid the death penalty that God's law demanded for sin.[26] It is our union with Christ by faith that saves us from the curse and condemnation of God's law.

Just as in Christ you died to sin, "you also died to the law through the body of Christ. . . . But now, by dying to what once bound us [both sin and the law] we have been released from the law so that we might serve in the new way of the Spirit, and not in the old way of the written code [that is, the law]."[27]

Just as we were bound and shackled by sin, so also we were bound and shackled by the law. We were "in slavery" under the law. "We were held prisoners by the law, locked up until faith should be revealed."[28] But Christ has set us free from the curse, the power, and the condemnation of the law. This is the "glorious freedom of the children of God!"[29] "It is for freedom that Christ has set us free. Do not let yourselves be burdened again by a yoke of slavery. But by faith we eagerly await through the Spirit the righteousness for which we hope."[30]

If our hope of righteousness is in our ability to keep God's law, we are doomed, for we have no righteousness of our own. But thanks be to God! Our hope of righteousness is in Jesus Christ our Lord—who is not only the author and the perfector of our faith—but he himself is our righteousness.[31] The Son of God came into this world to do what the law could not do for us: "to enable us to serve him without fear, in holiness, and righteousness before him all our days."[32]

God has reconciled us to himself by Christ's death, to present us holy in his sight, blameless and perfect in Christ—if we continue to believe, standing firm in our faith, "not moved from the hope held out in the gospel."[33] We are free from accusation because God's holy law—that justly accused us—was nailed to the cross of Christ, its power to condemn vanishing as Christ poured out his soul unto death.[34]

> "Christ is the end of the law, so that there may be righteousness for everyone who believes. There is therefore now no condemnation for those who are in Christ Jesus!"[35]

Freedom from Death

Even Moses died and was buried—for "what man can live and not see death, or save himself from the power of the grave?"[36] The holy law of God, which Moses loved, had no power to save him, or any other person, from death—the final dungeon for all mankind. But "what the law was powerless to do, . . . God did by sending his own Son," who "suffered death, so that by the grace of God he might taste death for everyone."[37] Like Moses, Jesus Christ died and was buried. His battered, broken body was taken off the cross and sealed in a tomb. But neither death nor the grave could hold him. "He was declared with power to be the Son of God by his resurrection from the dead."[38]

Long before Christ himself brought words of eternal life, God gave hope to the world through the promise of victory over death. "The Lord Almighty . . . will destroy the shroud that enfolds all peoples, the sheet that covers all nations. He will swallow up death forever."[39] "The people walking in darkness have seen a great light; on those living in the land of the shadow of death a light has dawned. For to us a child is born, to us a son is given."[40] God promised that a Saviour—a human child, a baby boy of flesh and blood—would be born into this world to destroy death and deliver us all. He came into the world "so that by his death he might destroy him who holds the power of death—that is, the devil—and free those who all their lives were held in slavery by their fear of death."[41]

The Son of God came into this world to destroy the works of the devil. We read in the Bible, "The last enemy to be destroyed is death," and, "we know that since Christ was raised from the dead, he cannot die again; death no longer has mastery over him."[42] Rather, Christ has victory even over death. "Death has been swallowed up in victory. . . . The sting of death is sin, and the power of sin is the law. But thanks be to God! He gives us the victory through our Lord Jesus Christ," who came to free us from the power of them all—sin, the law, and death.[43]

Jesus testified concerning himself: "Just as the Father raises the dead and gives them life, even so the Son gives life to whom he is pleased to give it. . . . I tell you the truth, whoever hears my word and believes him who sent me has eternal life and will not be condemned; he has crossed over from death to life. I tell you the truth, a time is coming and has now come when the dead will hear the voice of the Son of God and those who hear will live. For as the Father has life in himself, so he has granted the Son to have life in himself."[44] Jesus has victory over death, and has the power to give us life that no one can take away from us. He declared, "I am the resurrection and the life. He who believes in me will live, even though he dies; and whoever lives and believes in me will never die."[45]

But how can we believe that we have crossed over from death to life when we know that everyone dies? Like everyone in the whole world, the person who believes in Jesus grows old and weak and sick—and then he dies. His final resting place is a sad grave in the cold ground with a tombstone declaring the certainty and finality of his death. How can this be, when Jesus has promised us everlasting life and victory over death?

Although Christ has saved us and freed us from sin, we know there is still a residue of "sin living in me."[46] Yes, we still live inside our "bodies of death," but, "if Christ is in you, your body is dead because of sin, yet your spirit is alive because of righteousness. And if the Spirit of him who raised Jesus from the dead is living in you, he who raised Christ from the dead will also give life to your mortal bodies."[47] One day our bodies—even the ones that have already disintegrated into dust—will be raised to everlasting life to share in Christ's glory. One day the whole world, "the creation itself, will be liberated from its bondage to decay and brought into the glorious freedom of the children of God."[48]

The final word for us is not death and the last glimpse of us is not a corpse in its grave. Christ will set free even our bodies from the bondage of death and decay, and our great hope is his promise to us of resurrection. We must live by faith, and not by sight, believing that one day our bodies will be raised to everlasting life and glory.[49] Jesus has the power to set us free from the terrors and tortures of death and hell, and so he commands us not to fear. Jesus, the one who loves us and gave himself for us, holds the keys to unlock our graves and to set us free forever!

> Jesus said, "Do not be afraid. I am the first and the last.
> I am the Living One; I was dead, and behold I am alive forever and ever!
> I hold the keys of death and hell."[50]

A Vision of Resurrection (Ezekiel 37:1–14)

I want to leave you with a vision of the resurrection of our bodies that the Lord gave to his prophet Ezekiel. The Spirit of the Lord set him in the middle of a valley. (Perhaps it was the valley of the shadow of death, for it was a valley full of bones.) The Lord led Ezekiel back and forth among these old, brittle bones and asked him if these bones could live. Then the Lord commanded Ezekiel to prophesy to these dead bones saying: "Dry bones, hear the word of the Lord! This is what the Sovereign Lord says to these bones: '. . . I will attach tendons to you and make flesh come upon you and cover you with skin; I will put breath in you and you will come to life. Then you will know that I am the Lord.'"

And as Ezekiel was speaking the word of God to these bones, he heard a strange rattling sound. The bones in the valley came together, bone attaching to bone, tendons and flesh appearing on them and skin covering them. But there was no breath in these bodies—they remained lifeless corpses. Then the Lord commanded Ezekiel to prophesy: "This is what the Sovereign Lord says: 'Come from the four winds, O breath, and breathe into these slain, that they may live.'" So Ezekiel prophesied as the Lord commanded him and breath entered them; they came to life and stood up on their feet—a vast army.

The Lord explained to Ezekiel that these bones were the whole house of Israel, who had given up hope during their exile. Without hope and without faith, the people themselves realized they were like dry bones scattered in a valley. God commanded Ezekiel to prophesy to them, saying, "This is what the Sovereign Lord says: 'O my people, I am going to open your graves and bring you up from them. . . . Then you, my people, will know that I am the Lord, when I open your graves and bring you up from them. I will put my Spirit in you and you will live.'" So shall the Lord open our graves and raise the dust of our bones into glorified beings who will live with him forever.

Our Future Hope

The book of Deuteronomy ends with the death of Moses and his unmarked grave. There is no resurrection. There is no rejoicing. This book ends with weeping and mourning, and the people moving on without Moses, since when we die, life in this world continues without us.

But Deuteronomy does not have the last word—it is only the fifth book of the Bible. In the last book we read these words of our future hope: "Now the dwelling of God is with men and he will live with them. They will be his people, and God himself will be with them and be their God. He will wipe every tear from their eyes. There will be no more death or mourning or crying or pain, for the old order of things has passed away."[51]

"Jesus says, 'I am coming soon.' Amen. Come Lord Jesus!

The grace of the Lord Jesus be with God's people. Amen."[52]

LESSON 17: TEACHERS GUIDE

The Glorious Freedom of the Children of God

What does this lesson have to do with Deuteronomy? I did not want to leave the children back in the old covenant, searching for the grave of Moses in the land of Moab, with the grieving of the Israelites being the last sound that they would hear. Deuteronomy is a book about the snares of sin, the curse of the law, and the grip of death on all people. Although there are glimmers of Christ's glorious gospel in this book, it seemed as if I would be leaving the children trapped in the valley of the shadow of death. I wanted them to know that Christ sets us free. "In my anguish I cried to the Lord, and he answered by setting me free. The Lord is with me; I will not be afraid."[53]

VISUAL AIDS:

This is a lesson about being set free. Pictures of people behind bars and barbed wire or photos of people being liberated from death camps would be useful for this lesson.

Also, I have a large rusty ring of antique keys, which look like the keys an old-time jailer would have carried. Talk to the children about how Jesus hold the keys of death and hell. He unlocks the prisons where the law, sin, and death held us captive.

MEMORY WORK:

> "To him who loves us and has freed us from our sins by his blood; . . . to him be glory and power forever and ever! Amen."
>
> Revelation 1:5–6

> "Christ is the end of the law, so that there may be righteousness for everyone who believes."
>
> Romans 10:4

Jesus said, "Do not be afraid. I am the First and the Last. I am the Living One; I was dead, and behold I am alive forever and ever! And I hold the keys of death and hell."

Revelation 1:18

REVIEW QUESTIONS:

1. Who are the children of God?
2. How are the children of God free?
3. Why was the Son of God sent into the world?
4. What does the Bible mean when it says that each one of us was a "slave to sin"?
5. How did Jesus free us from sin? Why did he do this?
6. When we are united to Christ by faith, sin is no longer the ruling force within our hearts. Who now is the controlling power working within us?
7. "I have been crucified with Christ and I no longer live, but Christ lives in me." What does this mean?
8. Why was Moses unable to keep the law of God? Who was the only person in the history of the world who perfectly kept the holy law of God?
9. The laws of the Lord last forever! How then can we say that in Christ we are no longer "under law" and that we have been "released from the law?"
10. How did Jesus fulfil all the laws of the Old Testament? How does that affect us?
11. Who is our accuser? What does he do? Who is our advocate? What does he do? Who is more powerful?
12. How are we "in slavery" and "held prisoners" under the law?
13. In what way does Christ set us free from the law of God?
14. How do we serve God in "the new way?" What was "the old way?"
15. What does it mean when we read in the Bible that Christ Jesus has become our righteousness and our holiness?

16. Moses died and was buried by God. Where is Moses' body now? Jesus also died and was buried. Where is Jesus' body now?
17. God promised to swallow up death forever by sending a Saviour to deliver us from death. Who was this Saviour? How did he conquer death?
18. Jesus promised us that whoever believes in him will not perish, but have eternal life. Why then do we still die?
19. We know that if we believe in Jesus, our spirits are with him in heaven as soon as we die. But what happens to our bodies? Will they also be raised from the dead? Upon what do we base this hope?
20. Who holds the keys of death and hell? Why is this a great comfort to us? In the face of death, what does Jesus command us to do?
21. The prophet Ezekiel had a vision of a valley. Can you describe what was in that valley and what took place there?

PRAYER:

Our heavenly Father, we thank you for the freedom that we have in Christ. Thank you that in him we have been delivered from the power of sin to destroy us, the power of the law to condemn us and the power of death to divide us from God for eternity. There can be no greater freedom in all the world. Help us, O Lord, to use our freedom to serve you with joy and praise all the days of our lives. Forgive us when we fail. Strengthen us when we struggle. Comfort us when we mourn. Lord, without you, we would be trapped forever, prisoners of sin and death, condemned justly by your holy law. But in your great Love and mercy and grace, you have saved us! You have granted us faith; you have given us life. Lord Jesus, you are our Saviour and we praise your holy name right now and forever. Amen and amen.

PSALMS TO SING:

These are just a few of the freedom songs:

116A . . . and 6; 22AB (1–3); 31EF; 32B (9,12,13); 32C; 34ABC; 49B; 51BE; 56; 64A (1,9); 66C (1, 3, 5); 71A; 102B; 116C; 138AB

About the Author

Nancy Ganz lives in her native land of Canada, helping her husband, Dr. Richard Ganz, in church-planting work and home-schooling their four daughters. She received her formal theological training from the University of Toronto prior to her conversion to Christ at L'Abri in the Netherlands. However, it has been the many years of Bible study since that time which has produced her *Herein Is Love* commentaries on the Old Testament. Currently, most of her time is spent studying the Scriptures, writing various books, and taking long walks along the country roads and woodland paths near her home.

NOTES

Introduction

1. Deuteronomy 31:12

2. Colossians 3:16

3. The Psalter I have used is *The Book of Psalms for Singing* originally published in 1973 by the Reformed Presbyterian Church of North America. To order this hymn book, contact Crown & Covenant Publications, 7408 Penn Ave., Pittsburgh, PA 15208, USA. www.crownandcovenant.com

Chapter 1: The Importance of Deuteronomy

1. Proverbs 30:5

2. 2 Timothy 3:16. God's people believe that "everything that was written in the past was written to teach us, so that through endurance and the encouragement of the Scriptures we might have hope." (Romans 15:4) It is also true that the Word of God is living and powerful. It is able to pierce into the core of our beings to transform us. "Sharper than any double-edged sword, it penetrates even to dividing soul and spirit. . . . It judges the thoughts and attitudes of the heart" (Hebrews 4:12).

3. 1 Corinthians 13:13

4. Deuteronomy 17:18–19. Phrases such as "the words of this law" and "this book of the law" may not refer exclusively to Deuteronomy, although they certainly include it. Throughout the Scriptures, "the law" can refer to the summary of God's law (the ten commandments), the book of Deuteronomy alone (in part or in its entirety), or all five books of Moses. When Jesus said, "Everything must be fulfilled that is written about me in the law of Moses, the Prophets and the Psalms"(Luke 24:44), the "law of Moses" included all five books of the Pentateuch—Genesis, Exodus, Leviticus, Numbers, and Deuteronomy.

5. Deuteronomy 27:1–8

6. Deuteronomy 31:9–13

7. Deuteronomy 31:24–26

8. Deuteronomy 34:10–12

9. As a prophet, Moses "spoke from God" as he was "carried along by the holy Spirit" (2 Peter 1:21). The words in Deuteronomy are inspired by God Himself. They

did not have their origin with any man, not even a great man like Moses. "No prophecy of Scripture came about by the prophet's own interpretation" (2 Peter 1:20). These words of Scripture in Deuteronomy are not the product of Moses' rumination or imagination, but of God's revelation!

10. Deuteronomy 29:29

11. Moses said to the people, "I will die in this land; I will not cross the Jordan; but you are about to cross over and take possession of the good land" (Deuteronomy 4:22).

12. Deuteronomy 11:8

13. Deuteronomy 18:15

14. Deuteronomy 18:18–19

15. John 6:14. Other people, when they heard Jesus' wonderful teaching, said the same thing: "Surely this man is the Prophet" (John 7:40)—the Prophet whom Moses had promised them. Others said, "He is the Messiah! He is the Christ" (John 7:41). Later, Jesus taught his disciples that it was written that the Messiah must suffer and die before he entered his glory. Where was it written? "Beginning with Moses, and then all the Prophets, [Jesus] explained to them what was said in all the Scriptures concerning himself" (Luke 24:27). The Christ, the Prophet, the Messiah—he was first proclaimed in the writings of Moses.

16. John 5:39–40, 46

17. When the tempter said, "If you are the Son of God, tell these stones to become bread," Jesus answered, "It is written: Man does not live on bread alone, but on every word that comes from the mouth of God." Where was this written? Deuteronomy 8:3. When the devil took him to the highest point of the temple and said, "If you are the Son of God, throw yourself down," Jesus answered, "It is also written: Do not put the LORD your God to the test." Where was this written? Deuteronomy 6:16. When the tempter took Jesus to a very high mountain to show him all the kingdoms of the world and their splendour, he said, "All this I will give you, if you will bow down and worship me." Jesus answered, "Away from me Satan! For it is written: Worship the LORD your God and serve him only." Where was this written? Deuteronomy 6:13. All three times the Son of God answered from the book of Deuteronomy! (See Matthew 4:1–11.)

18. Deuteronomy 17:18–19

19. Ephesians 6:12

20. Matthew 22:34–40; Mark 12:28–31. Jesus was quoting from Deuteronomy 6:5.

21. Deuteronomy 22:6, 7

22. Some environmentalists might find in this book a few appropriate quotes for protest signs: "Do not destroy [the] trees by putting an axe to them. . . . Do not cut them down" (Deuteronomy 20:19).

23. Psalm 103:7–8, 11
24. Deuteronomy 7:6; 14:2
25. Deuteronomy 7:6–12
26. Deuteronomy 23:5
27. 1 John 4:10

Chapter 2: Do Not Forget-Remembering Egypt

1. Deuteronomy 5:15; 6:12; 7:18
2. Deuteronomy 15:15; 16:12; 24:18
3. Deuteronomy 4:32–35, 39
4. Deuteronomy 5:6–8
5. Deuteronomy 10:17, 20–21
6. Deuteronomy 4:37
7. Deuteronomy 7:8
8. Deuteronomy 5:6
9. Deuteronomy 11:1–8
10. Deuteronomy 6:20–25
11. Deuteronomy 28:20–21, 58–59, 61–62
12. Deuteronomy 1:29, 30
13. Deuteronomy 7:17–19, 21. Again Moses said, "When you go to war against your enemies and see horses and chariots and an army greater than yours, do not be afraid of them, because the Lord your God, who brought you up out of Egypt, will be with you" (Deuteronomy 20:1).
14. Deuteronomy 10:17–19
15. Moses said, "Remember that you were slaves in Egypt and the Lord your God redeemed you from there. That is why I command you to do this" (Deuteronomy 24:18).
16. Deuteronomy 24:19–22
17. Deuteronomy 15:12–15
18. 1 John 4:19
19. Jesus said, "For God so loved the world that he gave his one and only Son, that whoever believes in him shall not perish, but have eternal life" (John 3:16), and, "I tell you the truth, whoever hears my word and believes him who sent me has eternal life and will not be condemned; he has crossed over from death to life" (John 5:24).

2. Jesus once said, "I have spoken to you of earthly things and you do not believe; how then will you believe if I speak of heavenly things?"

21. One day God's people would remember another deliverance, a greater deliverance—their salvation in Jesus Christ—and they would shout and sing for joy, "God has rescued us from the dominion of darkness and brought us into the kingdom of the

Son he loves, in whom we have redemption, the forgiveness of sins" (Colossians 1:13–14).

22. Exodus 20:11

23. God said, "Remember that you were slaves in Egypt and that the Lord your God brought you out of there with a mighty hand and an outstretched arm. Therefore the Lord your God has commanded you to observe the Sabbath Day" (Deuteronomy 5:15).

24. Deuteronomy 16:6

25. Deuteronomy 16:3

26. Jesus himself said, "If the Son sets you free, you will be free indeed" (John 8:36).

27. 1 Corinthians 5:7

28. Luke 22:19

29. "My father" meant their ancestor Jacob, who was a wanderer and a foreigner all his life, and whose name God changed to Israel, meaning "he wrestles with God."

30. Deuteronomy 26:1–2, 4–10

31. Perhaps they sang songs like Psalm 100 or 95.

32. "Christ has indeed been raised from the dead, the firstfruits of those who have fallen asleep. For since death came through a man, the resurrection of the dead comes also through a man. For as in Adam all die, so in Christ all will be made alive. But each in his own turn: Christ, the Firstfruits, then, when he comes [a second time], those who belong to him" (1 Corinthians 15:20–23); "He is the beginning and the firstborn from among the dead" (Colossians 1:18).

33. "If anyone is in Christ, he is a new creation. The old has gone; the new has come" (2 Corinthians 5:17). Jesus himself taught that another spiritual birth into this new humanity was necessary for us to enter heaven and live forever. "Flesh and blood cannot inherit the kingdom of God" (1 Corinthians 15:42–50). Jesus declared, "I tell you the truth, no one can enter the kingdom of God unless he is born of water and the Spirit. Flesh gives birth to flesh, but the Spirit gives birth to spirit. You should not be surprised at my saying: 'You must be born again'" (John 3:3–8)! The first time we are born we are just tiny babies as we emerge from our mothers' wombs. That amazing event happens just once in each person's lifetime and cannot be repeated. How then can we be born a second time? Jesus explained the process: It is by believing in the Son of God. "For God so loved the world that he gave his one and only Son, that whoever believes in him shall not perish but have eternal life" (John 3:16). That is how the Holy Spirit enters our hearts and makes us alive in Christ. However, when we believe in Jesus, our bodies stay exactly the same. We do not glow or fly or walk on water. In fact, our lives seem to be just ordinary lives and sometimes people doubt whether anything has happened at all. Our bodies get sick, weak, old, and eventually

they die. So, how then are we raised from the dead, and when? "Listen, I tell you a mystery. . . . We will all be changed—in a flash, in a twinkling of an eye, at the last trumpet. For the trumpet will sound, the dead will be raised imperishable, and we will be changed. For the perishable must clothe itself with the imperishable, and the mortal with immortality." When this happens, God's Word will be fulfilled: "Death has been swallowed up in victory" (Isaiah 25:8)! "Thanks be to God! He gives us the victory through our Lord Jesus Christ" (1 Corinthians 15:57).

34. "God's incomparably great power, which he exerted in Christ when he raised him from the dead, is the same power at work in us who are united to Christ by faith. "Because of his great LOVE for us, God, who is rich in mercy, made us alive with Christ even when we were dead in sins (Ephesians 2:4)."

35. "He chose to give us birth through the Word of Truth, that we might be a kind of firstfruits of all he created" (James 1:18).

36. Zephaniah 3:13

37. See Revelation 7:1–17; 14:1–5.

Chapter 3: Do Not Forget-Remembering the Desert

1. Also called Mount Sinai, but "Horeb" is the name used throughout Deuteronomy.

2. Deuteronomy 5:2, 4, 23–27

3. Deuteronomy 4:32–35, 39

4. Deuteronomy 4:9–10, 15–17, 23–24

5. Deuteronomy 33:3–4

6. "Praise the LORD. . . . He has revealed his Word to Jacob, his Laws . . . to Israel. He has done this for no other nation; they do not know his Laws" (Psalm 147:1, 19, 20).

7. Moses said, "The Lord wrote on these tablets what he had written before—the ten commandments he had proclaimed to you on the mountain, out of the fire, on the day of the assembly. And the Lord gave them to me. Then I came back down the mountain and put the tablets in the ark I had made, as the Lord commanded me and they are there now" (Deuteronomy 10:4–5).

8. Deuteronomy 1:19

9. Jeremiah 2:6

10. Deuteronomy 1:29–31

11. Deuteronomy 8:2

12. Deuteronomy 1:33

13. Deuteronomy 2:7

14. Deuteronomy 32:7, 10–12

15. Deuteronomy 2:36

16. Deuteronomy 3:21–22

17. Deuteronomy 2:7
18. Deuteronomy 8:15–18
19. Deuteronomy 8:4
20. One day the Son of God would say, "I tell you, do not worry about your life, what you will eat or drink; or about your body, what you will wear. Is not life more important than food, and the body more important than clothes? . . . Do not worry, saying, 'What shall we eat?' or 'What shall we drink?' or 'What shall we wear?' For the pagans run after all these things, and your heavenly Father knows that you need them. But seek first his kingdom and his righteousness, and all these things will be given to you as well. Therefore, do not worry" (Luke 6:25–34). The Israelites in the wilderness were a perfect example of how God provides for the physical needs of his people.
21. Deuteronomy 8:2–5
22. Proverbs 3:12
23. cf. Leviticus 23:33–43
24. Deuteronomy 16:17
25. Deuteronomy 16:13–15
26. Deuteronomy 1:26, 32, 43
27. Deuteronomy 9:23–24
28. Deuteronomy 1:34
29. Deuteronomy 9:7–8
30. Deuteronomy 11:6; 4:3; 9:22
31. 1 Corinthians 10:6–12
32. John 14:26

Chapter 4: The Secret of Success

1. Deuteronomy 4:1
2. Deuteronomy 11:22–25
3. Deuteronomy 4:39–40, italics mine
4.Deuteronomy 5:29, italics mine
5. Deuteronomy 5:32–33
6. Deuteronomy 32:46–47
7. Deuteronomy 28:1–2
8. Deuteronomy 4:5–9
9. Deuteronomy 28:1–2, 9–10, 13
10. Deuteronomy 6:1–2, 6–9
11. Deuteronomy 6:24–25
12. Deuteronomy 4:15–16, 19
13. Deuteronomy 4:23, 25–27. Again Moses said, "I command you today to love the LORD your God, to walk in his ways, and to keep his commands, decrees, and laws; then you will live and increase, and the LORD your God will bless you in the

land you are entering to possess. But if your heart turns away and you are not obedient, and if you are drawn away to bow down to other gods and worship them, I declare to you this day that you will not live long in the land you are crossing the Jordan to enter and possess" (Deuteronomy 30:16–18).

14. Deuteronomy 12:28, 32
15. Deuteronomy 8:6–14, 17–20
16. Deuteronomy 6:10–16, 18–19
17. Deuteronomy 11:12
18. Deuteronomy 11:16–17
19. Deuteronomy 29:9
20. Deuteronomy 26:16–19
21. Deuteronomy 10:12–13
22. Deuteronomy 7:11–14
23. Deuteronomy 30:11
24. Deuteronomy 31:16, 20–21
25. Deuteronomy 31:27, 29
26. Ecclesiastes 7:29
27. Jeremiah 17:9. How did this happen? "Sin entered the world through one man, and death through sin, and in this way death spread to all men, because all sinned" (Romans 5:12). Through the first man the whole human race had become corrupt.
28. Genesis 6:5, 11
29. Galatians 3:22
30. "There is no one righteous, not even one. There is no one who understands, no one who seeks for God. All have turned away" (Romans 3:11–12). "Not a word from their mouth can be trusted. Their heart is filled with destruction" (Psalm 5:9). "There is no one who does good. God looks down from heaven on the sons of men to see if there are any who understand, any who seek for God. Everyone has turned away; they have together become corrupt. There is no one who does good, not even one" (Psalm 53:1–3). "There is not a righteous man on earth, who does what is right and never sins" (Ecclesiastes 7:20).
31. Galatians 3:21
32. Ezekiel 2:3
33. See Ezekiel 2:5–7
34. "Jews and Gentiles alike are all under sin. There is no difference, for all have sinned and fall short of the glory of God" (Romans 3:9, 23).
35. Deuteronomy 9:4–5 NKJV, 9:6 NIV
36. Romans 3:2
37. Ezekiel 33:11

38. Romans 7:12. We know also that "the law is spiritual" (Romans 7:14) and that "the law of the LORD is perfect, reviving the soul . . . making wise the simple . . . giving joy to the heart . . . giving light to the eyes" (Psalm 19:7–8).

39. Romans 3:20; 7:7. In fact, "the law was added so that trespass might increase" (Romans 5:20). The law actually aroused man's sinful passions (Romans 7:5), because in his sinful human nature, man's desire and delight was to rebel against God and to break all the restraints of God's law. Sinful man detests God and glories in his rebellion against God and his law. So, "when the commandment came, sin sprang to life. . . . The very commandment that was intended to bring life actually brought death" (Romans 7:9–10), because sin in man's heart seized the opportunity afforded by the commandment to rebel against God by producing every kind of evil expressly forbidden by God. Thus one reason that the LORD gave his holy law was "in order that sin might be recognized as sin . . . and so that through the commandment sin might become utterly sinful" (Romans 7:13). What we were as fallen creatures would be abundantly clear!

40. Galatians 3:23

41. Luke 18:13; Romans 7:24

42. "The law was put in charge to lead us to Christ, that we might be justified by faith" (Galatians 3:24).

43. "God did not send his Son into the world to condemn the world, but to save the world through him" (John 3:17). "For God so loved the world that he gave his one and only Son, that whoever believes in him shall not perish, but have eternal life" (John 3:16).

44. John 6:40, 47

45. John 11:25

46. 1 John 3:1

47. Galatians 3:22

Chapter 5: The Ten Commandments . . . Again

1. At that time Jesus Christ said, "Do not think I have come to abolish the law or the prophets; I have not come to abolish them, but to fulfil them. I tell you the truth, until heaven and earth disappear, not the smallest letter, not the least stroke of the pen, will by any means disappear from the law until everything is accomplished" (Matthew 5:17–18).

2. Deuteronomy 6:4–5; Mark 12:29; Matthew 22:37; Matthew 22:38

3. Moses said, "It is on account of the wickedness of these nations that the Lord is going to drive them out before you" (Deuteronomy 9:4–5).

4. Deuteronomy 7:1–3, 16; 20:16–18

5. Deuteronomy 7:5–6, 25–26

6. Deuteronomy 12:2, 3

7. Deuteronomy 12:4–7, 14

8. Deuteronomy 12:29–31

9. Deuteronomy 18:9–13

10. Deuteronomy 13:1–8

11. Deuteronomy 17:2–7

12. Deuteronomy 13:12–18

13. See Deuteronomy 16:1–17

14. Tithing to the Lord was also an important part of worship. Moses told them, "Be sure to set aside a tenth of all that your fields produce each year" (Deuteronomy 14:22; see also Deuteronomy 26). In their sacrifices to God, the Israelites must be careful to offer the first and the best to God. To do otherwise would be to dishonour God. Moses said, "Do not sacrifice to the Lord your God an ox or a sheep that has any defect or flaw in it, for that would be detestable to him" (Deuteronomy 17:1).

15. Mark 12:28–31, italics mine

16. Matthew 22:40

17. Matthew 7:12, italics mine

18. Jesus said, "Love your enemies; do good to those who hate you; bless those who curse you; pray for those who mistreat you. . . . *Do to others as you would have them do to you.* Then your reward will be great and you will be children of the Most High, because he is kind to the ungrateful and wicked. Be merciful, just as your Father is merciful" (Luke 6:27–36). Jesus also said, "A new command I give you: *love one another.* As I have loved you, so you must love one another" (John 13:34). Again Jesus said, "My command is this: *love one another,* as I have loved you" (John 15:12). A third time Jesus said, "This is my command: *love one another*" (John 15:17). We read in the New Testament: "If you really keep the royal law found in the Scripture—'*love your neighbour as yourself*'—you are doing right" (James 2:8). (All italics mine.)

19. Romans 13:8–10, italics mine

20. Moses commanded them to strive to be a just people and a holy nation, telling them, "Follow justice and justice alone" (Deuteronomy 16:20).

21. Romans 2:14–15

22. God says to Israel, "Let justice roll on like a river, righteousness like a never-failing stream" (Amos 5:24).

23. If you want to have 20:20 vision, obey Proverbs 20:20— or you will be plunged into complete darkness and blindness!

24. Proverbs 1:8; 15:20; 17:21; 20:20; 30:17. Proverbs has many other references to honouring one's father and mother: "My son, keep your father's commands and do not forsake your mother's teaching" (6:20). "A wise son brings joy to his father, but a foolish son brings grief to his mother" (10:1). "A foolish son is his father's ruin" (19:13). "He who robs his father and drives out his mother is a son who brings shame and

disgrace" (19:26). "Listen to your father, who gave you life, and do not despise your mother when she is old. …The father of a righteous man has great joy; he who has a wise son delights in him. May your father and mother be glad; may she who gave you birth rejoice" (23:22, 24–25).

25. That is, they shall take him to court and testify against him.

26. Deuteronomy 21:18–21

27. These proverbs and laws are speaking about adult sons and daughters, not boys and girls who are still learning and being trained in righteousness.

28. Matthew 15:4

29. Philippians 2:8

30. Luke 2:51

31. See John 2:1–11; 19:25–27

32. Romans 1:31

33. Ephesians 6:1–3; Colossians 3:20

34. God's law was, "You are to take life for life, eye for eye, tooth for tooth, hand for hand, foot for foot, burn for burn, wound for wound, bruise for bruise" (Exodus 21:23–25. See also Leviticus 24:19–20; Deuteronomy 19:21).

35. Genesis 9:5–6

36. Later, as their nation grew in size and the LORD enlarged their territory, Moses instructed them to establish more cities of refuge.

37. Deut 19:4–7;10

38. Deuteronomy 19:11–13

39. Deuteronomy 22:8

40. See Deuteronomy 21:28–36.

41. Matthew 5:21, italics mine

42. Luke 6:27–29

43. Luke 23:34

44. John 13:34

45. Revelation 21:8; 22:15

46. Romans 1:18, 29

47. Galatians 5:19–22

48. We should no longer live as slaves to our sinful nature, but as grateful children of God, who love because of the love we have been given. "At one time we too were foolish, disobedient, deceived, and enslaved by all kinds of passions and pleasures. We lived in malice and envy, being hated and hating one another. But when the kindness and love of God our Saviour appeared, he saved us, not because of righteous things we had done, but because of his mercy" (Titus 3:3–5). "Dear friends, since God so loved us, we also ought to love one another" (1 John 4:11).

49. God's kind of love is freely given even if we are not loved in return. "Bless

those who persecute you; bless and do not curse. . . . Do not repay anyone evil for evil. Be careful to do what is right in the eyes of everybody. If it is possible, as far as it depends on you, live at peace with everyone. Do not take revenge, my friends . . . On the contrary, if your enemy is hungry, feed him; if he is thirsty, give him something to drink. . . . Do not be overcome by evil, but overcome evil with good. He who loves his fellow man has fulfilled the law" (Romans 12:14, 17–21; 13:8).

50. Ephesians 4:31–5:2

51. Other sexual sins, such as homosexuality or bestiality, were also capital offenses incurring the death penalty. See Leviticus 20:13, 15.

52. Leviticus 20:10; Deuteronomy 22:22

53. Matthew 5:27–28

54. Matthew 23:27–28

55. God makes a husband and wife one, uniting them in both body and spirit, because he is seeking godly offspring. The purpose of the marriage union is to bring forth children for God.

56. See Matthew 19:3–9.

57. God commanded, "Husbands, love your wives just as Christ loved the church and gave Himself up for her" (Ephesians 5:25). This means a husband is to cherish his wife and adore her; he is to protect her and provide for her and even sacrifice himself for her.

58. Deuteronomy 24:1

59. Malachi 2: 16; 13–15

60. Matthew 19:9

61. Ephesians 5:3–6, 15. When we live in purity, that is pleasing to our Lord. "It is God's will that you should be sanctified: that you should avoid sexual immorality; that each of you should learn to control his own body in a way that is holy and honourable, not in passionate lust like the heathen, who do not know God" (1 Thessalonians 4:3–5).

62. Sexual immorality is often listed in the New Testament as one of the things our sinful hearts run after, and something that does not belong in the life of one who is the LORD's. "Live by the Spirit, and you will not gratify the desires of the sinful nature. The acts of the sinful nature are obvious: sexual immorality, impurity, and debauchery. I warn you that those who live like this will not inherit the kingdom of God. Those who belong to Christ Jesus have crucified the sinful nature with its passions and desires" (See Galatians 5:16–24). "Since, then, you have been raised with Christ, set your hearts on things above. Set your minds on things above, not on earthly things. Put to death, therefore, whatever belongs to your earthly nature: sexual immorality, impurity, lusts, evil desires. . . . Because of these the wrath of God is coming" (Colossians 3:1–2, 5–6).

63. 1 Corinthians 6:18–20

64. Deuteronomy 22:1, 3

65. Deuteronomy 25:13–16

66. Deuteronomy 19:14. The penalty for theft was restitution, that is, paying back more than what was taken. The only time stealing was a capital offence was when a person was stolen—kidnapping. “The kidnapper must die. You must purge the evil from among you” (Deuteronomy 24:7).

67. See Deuteronomy 14:22–29.

68. Deuteronomy 15:1, 7–11

69. Matthew 6:19–20, 24. Jesus continued, telling us that we must trust God to take care of our earthly needs, “Therefore I tell you, do not worry about your life, what you will eat or drink; or about your body, what you will wear. Is not life more important than food, and the body more important than clothes? The pagans run after all these things, and your heavenly Father knows that you need them. But seek first his kingdom and his righteousness, and all these things will be given to you as well” (Matthew 6:25–26, 32–33).

70. Luke 6:38

71. Mark 10:17–21. See also Matthew 19:16–21. Sadly, this man was not willing to obey Jesus. The story continues, “When the man heard this, his face fell and he went away sad, because he had great wealth. Then Jesus exclaimed, “I tell you the truth, it is hard for a rich man to enter the kingdom of heaven!” When the disciples heard this they asked, “Who then can be saved?” Jesus looked at them and said, “With man this is impossible, but with God all things are possible” (Mark 10:22–27).

72. 1 Corinthians 6:10

73. Ephesians 4:28

74. 2 Corinthians 9:6–8, 11

75. Leviticus 19:11, 15–16

76. Proverbs 6:16, 19

77. Proverbs 24:28; 10:18; 11:9; 21:23, 28. Proverbs also describes the people who practice such dishonesty: “A truthful witness gives honest testimony, but a false witness tells lies. Truthful lips endure forever, but a lying tongue lasts only a moment” (Proverbs 12:17, 19). “A truthful witness saves lives, but a false witness is deceitful” (Proverbs 14:25). “A false witness will not go unpunished, and he who pours out lies will not go free. He who pours out lies will perish” (Proverbs 19:5, 9). “Like a club or a sword or a sharp arrow is the man who gives false testimony against his neighbour” (Proverbs 25:18).

78. Deuteronomy 19:15–21. It was not just witnesses who must guard truth carefully. Judges and jurors not pervert justice by taking bribes, which is also a crime. In Deuteronomy Moses commanded: “Appoint judges and officials for each of your tribes

in every town the LORD your God is giving you, and they shall judge the people fairly. Do not pervert justice or show partiality. Do not accept a bribe, for a bribe blinds the eyes of the wise and twists the words of the righteous. Follow justice and justice alone, so that you may live and possess the land that the LORD your God is giving you" (Deuteronomy 16:18–20).

79. John 8:44

80. Again and again Jesus said, "Verily, verily I say unto you." Again and again Jesus said, "I tell you the truth . . . I tell you the truth . . . I tell you the truth." (See Matthew 5:18, 26; 6:2, 5, 16; 8:10; 10:15, 23, 42; and many, many more.)

81. Isaiah 53:9. Jesus said, "I am the way and the truth and the life. No one comes to the Father except through me" (John 14:6).

82. Revelation 1:5; 3:7, 14; 9:11

83. Revelation 22:15

84. Revelation 21:8

85. 2 Corinthians 4:2; Ephesians 4:15, 22–25.

86. "The lamp of the LORD searches the spirit of a man; it searches out his inmost being" (Proverbs 20:27).

87. Habakkuk 2:9, NIV and KJV

88. Mark 7:20–23

89. Luke 12:15, NIV and KJV

90. Mark 8:36, KJV. Jesus himself faced that very temptation. The devil took him to a high mountain and showed him in an instant all the kingdoms of the world and their splendour—not only the countless vistas of natural beauty, but also all the power and wealth and glory of these nations. This temptation was of such magnitude that it is beyond human ability to comprehend it all, but the temptation was very simple in its design: the devil was hoping to find in Christ a covetous heart so Satan's fiery arrow could ignite it into a burning desire to own the whole world—a desire which then would give birth to sin. "All this I will give you," said the devil. "It has been given to me and I can give it to anyone I want." In some ways it was a legitimate offer. Satan was "the prince of this world" (John 12:31; 14:30; 16:11) and "the god of this age" (2 Corinthians 4:4), and he was offering his kingdom to Christ. "If you worship me, it will all be yours," promised the devil. "Just bow down and worship me and the whole world will belong to you." But Christ drove the prince of demons away from him with a word, commanding, "Away from me, Satan! For it is written: 'Worship the Lord your God and serve him only'"(Deuteronomy 6:13). Then the devil left Jesus for a short season, hoping to find a better opportunity to tempt and trap the Son of God (See Matthew 4:1–10; Luke 4:1–13).

91. Ephesians 5:5–6. See also 1 Corinthians 6:10, and Colossians 3:5–6.

92. 1 Timothy 6:6–11

93. Hebrews 13:5–6, quoting from Deuteronomy 31:6.

94. Philippians 4:11–13

95. Psalms 1:1–2; 40:4; 112:1; 119:1–2; 128:1; 2:12

96. If you prefer, you could use the version of this command found in Luke's gospel: Q. Of all the commandments, which is the most important? A. Jesus answered: "The most important one is this: Hear, O Israel, the Lord our God, the Lord is one. Love the Lord your God with all your heart and with all your soul and with all your mind and with all your strength. The second is this: Love your neighbour as yourself. There is no commandment greater than these" (Luke 12:29–31).

Chapter 6: Prophecies of Victory

1. Deuteronomy 19:1

2. Deuteronomy 7:18–19. Moses continues, "The Lord your God will do the same to all the peoples you now fear. Do not be terrified by them, for the Lord your God, who is among you, is a great and awesome God. The Lord your God will drive out those nations before you. . . . The Lord your God will deliver them over to you, throwing them into great confusion until they are destroyed. He will give their kings into your hand, and you will wipe out their names from under heaven. No one will be able to stand up against you. You will destroy them" (Deuteronomy 7:21–24).

3. Deuteronomy 9:1–3. Again Moses said, "You will cross the Jordan River and you will settle in the land the LORD your God is giving you as an inheritance, and he will give you rest from all your enemies around you so that you will live in safety" (Deuteronomy 12:10). "The LORD your God will cut off before you the nations you are about to invade and dispossess" (Deuteronomy 12:29). Victory was certain, because this was the Word of the LORD!

4. Trusting in God's LOVE brings great courage and comfort. The Israelites could hope and trust in that love because God's LOVE is not fickle—not here today, gone tomorrow. God's LOVE is a lasting love, enduring for a thousand generations. The Bible says over and over that God's LOVE endures forever. In Deuteronomy Moses declared to the Israelites, "The LORD did not set his affection on you and choose you because you were more numerous than other peoples. But it was because the LORD *loved* you and kept the oath he swore to your forefathers. . . . Know therefore that the LORD your God is God. He is the faithful God, keeping his covenant of LOVE to a thousand generations of those who love him and keep his commandments" (Deuteronomy 7:7–9, italics mine).

5. Deuteronomy 4:37–38, italics mine

6. Deuteronomy 10:14–15

7. See Romans 8:37

8. Deuteronomy 20:2–4

9. Deuteronomy 31:1–6

10. Luke 12:32

11. Revelation 17:14

12. Jesus said, "In this world you will have trouble. But take heart! I have overcome the world" (John 16:33). "Everyone who believes that Jesus is the Christ is born of God and . . . everyone born of God overcomes the world. This is the victory that has overcome the world, even our faith! Who is it that overcomes the world? Only he who believes that Jesus is the Son of God" (1 John 5:1, 4–5). Christ's followers are the ones who, in him, will overcome this present world and will inherit the new heavens and the new earth (See Revelation 21:7).

13. 1 Corinthians 15:57

14. Deuteronomy 31:6

15. Matthew 28:20, italics mine

16. It is written in God's own Word that "God so *loved* the world that he gave his one and only Son, that whoever believes in him shall not perish but have eternal life" (John 3:16, italics mine).

17. Romans 8:35, 37–39, italics mine

Chapter 7:The Promise of the Prophet

1. See Genesis 3:15

2. Genesis 12:3

3. Genesis 26:4

4. Genesis 28:14. When God spoke to him, Jacob was sleeping on the ground with a stone for a pillow, dreaming of the angels of God ascending and descending on a staircase between heaven and earth!

5. Genesis 49:10

6. Deuteronomy 18:15

7. Deuteronomy 18:16–19

8. Luke 3:15. The people were asking John the Baptist who he was and he said freely, "I am not the Messiah." "Then who are you?" they asked. "Are you the prophet?" John answered, "No." He was not the prophet promised by Moses. "Then who are you?" they pressed. John replied that he was a voice, calling in the desert: "Prepare the way for the Lord. . . . And all mankind will see God's salvation" (See John 1:19–27)! Who was John the Baptist? He was "the voice," promised in Isaiah, who would prepare the way for someone greater than himself. This then was John's message: "I baptize you with water. But one more powerful than I will come. . . . He will baptize you with the Holy Spirit and with fire" (Luke 3:16).

9. John 1:34

10. See John 7:40–41

11. John 1:45

12. John 6:14

13. Acts 3:22. Stephen, the church's first martyr, also referred to Jesus when he quoted from this passage just before he was stoned to death (See Acts 7:37).

14. John 5:46

15. Deuteronomy 18:15–19

16. "In the beginning was the Word, and the Word was with God, and the Word was God. He was with God in the beginning. The Word became flesh and made his dwelling among us" (John 1:1–2, 14).

17. Hebrews 1:1, 3

18. Mark 9:7

19. John 3:34–36

20. John 12:44–45, 49–50

21. John 14:24.

22. Psalm 40:7–10. At the beginning of his public teaching ministry, Jesus was handed the scroll of the prophet Isaiah to read in his home synagogue. Unrolling the scroll, Jesus found the place where it was written, "The Spirit of the Lord is upon me, because he has anointed me to preach the good news to the poor; he has sent me to proclaim freedom for the prisoners and recovery of sight for the blind, to release the oppressed, and to proclaim the year of the Lord's favour" (Isaiah 61:1–2). Then he declared to the people, "Today this Scripture is fulfilled in your hearing" (Luke 4:21).

23. John 10:30

24. As Isaiah the prophet lamented, "Woe is me! I am ruined! For I am a man of unclean lips, and I live among a people of unclean lips" (Isaiah 6:5). But Jesus was not unclean like the rest of mankind. He was perfectly pure, a man without sin; he did nothing wrong, "nor was any deceit in his mouth" (Isaiah 53:9). Every word that came from the lips of Jesus was a word of grace and truth (John 1:17).

25. When the LORD appeared to Moses from within a burning bush and told him, "Go—I am sending you to Pharaoh to bring my people the Israelites out of Egypt," Moses was concerned that the people would not believe him or listen to him. The LORD gave Moses miraculous signs to perform before all the people, but still Moses was afraid that he was unable to do this great task. Moses said, "O LORD, I have never been eloquent, neither in the past nor since you have spoken to your servant. I am slow of speech and tongue." The LORD answered Moses, "Who gave man his mouth? Is it not I, the LORD? Now go. I will help you speak and will teach you what to say." But still Moses did not want to go and pleaded with the LORD, who agreed to send Moses' brother Aaron to speak for him. This was Israel's greatest prophet! It is hard to believe that Moses was so fearful that he needed his brother to speak for him. The LORD would speak to Moses and then Moses would speak to Aaron and then finally Aaron would speak God's Word to

the people. Later in his ministry, Moses would speak directly to the people himself. But still he was just a man speaking the words of God. Again and again we read of the LORD speaking to Moses and then Moses declaring, "This is what the LORD says . . . "

26. Deuteronomy 34:10–12

27. Matthew 11:2–6

28. "Many people saw the miraculous signs he was doing and believed in his name" (John 2:23). "After the people saw the miraculous signs that Jesus did, they began to say, 'Surely this is the Prophet who is to come into the world'" (John 6:14). People also said, "When the Christ comes, will he do more miraculous signs than this man" (John 7:31)?

29. John 10:25, 37

30. Hebrews 3:3

31. See Philippians 2:5–8

32. Hebrews 2:14, 17

33. Deuteronomy 18:14, 20–22

34. See John 2:18–22

35. See also Matthew 12:38–41; Mark 8:31–32.

36. Jesus "was declared with power to be the Son of God by his resurrection from the dead" (Romans 1:4).

Chapter 8: Renewal of the Covenant

1. Deuteronomy 29:10, 12. Moses said, "I am making this covenant with its oath not only with you who are standing here with us today in the presence of the Lord our God, but also with those who are not here today" (Deuteronomy 29:14–15).

2. Deuteronomy 7:9

3. Exodus 19:5–8; 24:3, 7–8

4. Deuteronomy 26:16–19

5. Deuteronomy 27:9

6. Deuteronomy 29:4, 6. Later, Isaiah and Jesus would both say the same thing about Israel. "Seeing, you do not see, and hearing you do not hear" (Isaiah 6:9–10; Matthew 13:14).

7. Deuteronomy 29:16–18

8. Deuteronomy 29:19–21

9. Deuteronomy 29:23–28

10. Moses said, "The secret things belong to the LORD our God." Yes, there are many mysteries about which we have no knowledge, and there are many questions for which we have no answers—but God's covenant, and the necessity of not breaking that covenant, was not in that category!

11. Hebrews 3:12

Chapter 9: The Tale of Two Mountains

1. Deuteronomy 11:30
2. Deuteronomy 27:2–4, 8
3. Deuteronomy 27:5–6
4. Deuteronomy 11:26–28
5. Numbers 6:24–26
6. Deuteronomy 27:15
7. "For God did not send his son into the world to condemn the world, but to save the world through him" (John 3:17).
8. See Matthew 5:1–12
9. Galatians 3:13
10. John 1:16–17
11. See Ephesians 1:3–6

Chapter 10: Blessing or Cursing

1. Deuteronomy 29:22–28
2. Deuteronomy 30:1–10
3. Deuteronomy 30:11, 14

Chapter 11: A Choice

1. Genesis 2:16–17
2. And thus "sin entered the world through one man, and death through sin, and in this way death came to all men, because all sinned" (Romans 5:12).
3. Genesis 3:22–24
4. Deuteronomy 30:15–18
5. Deuteronomy 30:19–20
6. Revelation 2:7
7. Deuteronomy 6:5; 11:22; 30:10, 6
8. See Luke 23:33–33.
9. Jesus said, "I am the resurrection and the life. He who *believes* in me will live, even though he dies; and whoever lives and believes in me will never die" (John 11:25–26, italics mine).
10. Ephesians 2:5, 8
11. John 3:14–18
12. John 5:24; 6:40, 47
13. Deuteronomy 30:11–12
14. Jesus said, "I am the way and the truth and the life" (John 14:6).
15. Luke 24:25, John 20:27
16. Deuteronomy 30:14

17. Romans 10:6–10; Joel 2:32. Jesus also reminded us, "Let not your hearts be troubled. Believe in God; believe also in me" (John 14:1 KJV).

Chapter 12: A New Leader

1. Deuteronomy 31:2. It was not because of his age, but because of his sin, that he could not go with Israel into the Promised Land. God had said to him, "You shall not cross the Jordan." Numbers 20:1–13 records the story of Moses' disobedience.

2. Deuteronomy 31:1:3, 6, 8

3. Numbers 11:28

4. Exodus 24:12–14

5. In fact, Joshua was the one who heard the noise first. He was a soldier and thought it was the sound of fighting. He told Moses, "There is the sound of war in the camp"—but Moses replied, "It is not the sound of victory; it is not the sound of defeat. It is the sound of singing that I hear." Soon enough their eyes saw what was happening: the people were dancing before a detestable idol (Exodus 32:15–20).

6. Exodus 33:11

7. Exodus 17:8–16

8. The ten faithless spies were struck down with a deadly a plague before the LORD, but Joshua and the other faithful spy, Caleb, survived. Numbers chapters 12 and 13 tell the full story of Caleb and Joshua's faith in the Lord.

9. Numbers 14:6, 30, 36–38; 32:12

10. Numbers 34:16–17

11. Numbers 13:16 "Joshua" was also the name that God chose for his only begotten Son. God said, "You are to give him the name Jesus, because he will save his people from their sins" (Matthew 1:21). Jesus is the Greek form of the Hebrew name Joshua ("The LORD is salvation!").

12. Deuteronomy 3:27–28. Moses had pleaded with God to be allowed to enter the land, but the LORD was angry with Moses and would not listen to him. "That is enough," the LORD had said. "Do not speak to me anymore about this matter." Moses could climb to the top of a mountain to view the land, but he could not enter it.

13. Numbers 27:12–23

14. Deuteronomy 34:9

15. Deuteronomy 31:7–8

16. Deuteronomy 31:14, 23, italics mine

Chapter 13: A Book, a Song, and a Blessing

1. Deuteronomy 31:24

2. Deuteronomy 31:26

3. Deuteronomy 31:9–13

4. This law of the LORD was to be stored not only in the heart of the nation (that

is, in the most holy place of God's Tabernacle)—these words were to be stored in all the hearts of the nation as well. God's Word was to be carefully treasured in every person's heart, so that the living Word of the LORD might live in them and give them life!

5. Isaiah 40:8

6. Deuteronomy 31:15–19

7. Deuteronomy 31:26–28

8. See Deuteronomy 33:6–24. There were twelve tribes of Israel, but Moses only mentioned eleven. Which tribe was missing? Simeon, the second-born son of Jacob. We do not know why Simeon was excluded from the blessing of Moses, but we do know that Jacob himself cursed the anger and fury of both Simeon and Levi. Their father Jacob said, "Simeon and Levi are brothers; their swords are weapons of violence. . . . Cursed be their anger, so fierce, and their fury, so cruel. I will scatter them in Jacob and disperse them in Israel" (Genesis 49:5–7). There was no territory for Levi in the land of Israel, because they were scattered throughout the tribes, and Simeon's territorial allotment was eventually absorbed by Judah.

9. Matthew 4:14–16; Isaiah 9:1–2

10. See Deuteronomy 33:26–29 for the full text of this wonderful final blessing.

Chapter 14: The Death of Moses

1. Deuteronomy 32:49–50

2. Psalm 90:17

3. Deuteronomy 34:10–12

4. I myself was converted to Christ and saved from my sins through the preaching of Moses!

5. Psalm 90:9–10

6. Even on the day he died and entered into his rest, the devil disputed with God's angels about the body of Moses (Jude 9)! But Satan had no claim on him—not even on his corpse. Once again God prevailed in protecting his servant. Moses' body was safely hidden on earth, and his soul was alive in heaven, securely hidden in Christ with God.

7. Hebrews 11:27

8. After Moses' death, the Israelites stayed on the east side of the Jordan River, grieving the loss of their leader for thirty days—until the time of weeping and mourning was over—before they marched off to battle in the land which God had given them, and to which Moses had brought them.

9. Deuteronomy 34:4

10. Deuteronomy 32:51–52

11. Psalm 90:13–15

12. 2 Timothy 4:6–8

13. Hebrews 3:5

Chapter 15: One Greater Than Moses

1. Hebrews 3:3, 5–6
2. John 1:17
3. One of the songs Moses wrote rejoiced in the fact that before the world was made, God existed. From all eternity to all eternity, God was and is and will be—and therefore all generations of people, as they are born and as they die, can find shelter in the eternal God. "Lord . . . from everlasting to everlasting you are God!" Psalm 90:2
4. Genesis 3:19
5. Psalm 90:3, 9–10
6. Psalm 22:15–16; 16:1, 9–10
7. Revelation 1:17–18
8. Romans 1:4; Hebrews 7:16
9. Deuteronomy 52:51; Numbers 20:12
10. Psalm 22:1–3
11. Luke 23:46
12. Deuteronomy 34:10–12
13. Matthew 11:5–6
14. John 1:4, italics mine

Chapter 16: A New and Living Way

1. Deuteronomy 31:16, 20
2. "All your commands are true. You established them to last forever. All your words are true; all your righteous laws are eternal" (Psalm 119:151–152, 160).
3. Hebrews 8:7, 13
4. Psalm 119:7, italics mine
5. Romans 7:12
6. Ezekiel 16:59
7. Ezekiel 16:60–62
8. Isaiah 42:8–9
9. God said, "Here is my servant, whom I uphold, my chosen one, in whom I delight. I will put my Spirit on him and he will bring justice to the nations. . . . In faithfulness he will bring forth justice; he will not falter till he establishes justice on earth" (Isaiah 42:1–4).
10. Ezekiel 37:25
11. Zechariah 9:9–10
12. Isaiah 53:5. "We have peace with God through our Lord Jesus Christ." (Romans 5:1). Through the prophet Isaiah, God spoke to his faithful servant long before his arrival on earth. God said to him, "I, the Lord, have called you in righteousness. I will take hold of your hand. I will keep you and I will make you to be a covenant for the people and a light for the Gentiles, to open eyes that are blind, to free captives

from prison and to release from the dungeon those who sit in darkness" (Isaiah 42:6–7). Again the Lord gave this prophetic word to his servant: "I will make you to be a covenant for the people; . . . to say to the captives, 'Come out,' and to those in darkness, 'Be free'" (Isaiah 49:8–9)! And before his crucifixion Jesus said, "This is my blood of the new covenant, which is poured out for many for the forgiveness of sins" (Matthew 26:28).

13. Ezekiel 37:23–24, 26. Jesus was the holy Son of God, sent from heaven, to negotiate everlasting peace between God and man through the covenant of peace, established in his own precious blood. "For God was pleased . . . through him to reconcile to himself all things . . . by making peace through his blood shed on the cross" (Colossians 1:20). This was indeed an everlasting covenant. "'Though the mountains be shaken and the hills removed, yet my unfailing Love for you will not be shaken, nor my covenant of peace be removed,' says the Lord, who has compassion on you" (Isaiah 54:10).

14. "The way of the wicked is like deep darkness" (Proverbs 4:19), but Jesus said, "I am the light of the world. Whoever follows me will never walk in darkness, but will have the light of life" (John 8:12).

15. The word of Christ himself was spoken through the prophet Zechariah: "Because of the blood of my covenant with you, I will free your prisoners from the waterless pit"(Zechariah 9:9–11)—from the dry, dead wasteland of their own hard hearts and from the horrors of hell. In the new covenant, Christ would set the prisoners free, to be refreshed and renewed with the water of life Jesus said, "If anyone is thirsty, let him come to me and drink. Whoever believes in me, . . . streams of living water will flow from within him"—and by this Christ meant the Holy Spirit (John 7:37).

16. Malachi 3:1. The name Malachi means "messenger." This prophet was the last messenger that God sent to speak his word in the old covenant Scriptures. Like all God's other prophets, he bore witness to the Messiah, announcing the anointed one who was no longer in the distant future, but was now close at hand.

17. 1 Timothy 2:5–6; Hebrews 9:15

18. Isaiah 55:3, 6–7

19. 2 Corinthians 3:6. Paul goes on to exclaim, "Now if the ministry that brought death, which was engraved with letters upon stone, came with glory, . . . will not the ministry of the Spirit be even more glorious? If the ministry that condemns men is glorious, how much more glorious is the ministry that brings righteousness! For what was glorious has no glory now in comparison with the surpassing glory. And if what was fading away came with glory, how much greater is the glory of that which lasts" (2 Corinthians 3:7–10). The new covenant that gives us everlasting life and righteousness is glorious indeed!

20. Leviticus 18:4.

21. Isaiah 59:9, 12. The prophet continues his lament, saying, "Our offenses are ever with us, and we acknowledge our iniquities: rebellion and treachery against the LORD, turning our backs on our God, fomenting oppression and revolt, uttering lies our hearts have conceived. So justice is driven back, and righteousness stands at a distance" (Isaiah 59:12–14).

22. Romans 3:20. We simply cannot do it. From our birth, from our very conception, we are all sinful by nature. "Surely I was sinful at birth, sinful from the time my mother conceived me" (Psalm 51:5). Like the rest of mankind, each one of us is from birth, by nature, an object of God's wrath. We cannot establish our own righteousness by our works—not even by our best desires and efforts at keeping God's holy law. It is arrogant to even think that our pitiable attempts at making ourselves righteous would find favour in the sight of a God who is perfect in holiness!

23. Leviticus 18:5

24. He was the only man who, according to God's law, could have bypassed death, based on his own merit, his own accomplishment of complete obedience and perfect righteousness. But Jesus chose to give himself over to death so that we might have life. "Surely he took up our infirmities and carried our sorrows. . . . He was pierced for our transgressions and crushed for our iniquities. The punishment that brought us peace was upon him, and by his wounds we are healed. We all, like sheep, have gone astray; each of us has turned to his own way—and the LORD has laid on him the iniquity of us all" (Isaiah 53:4–6). Christ, the holy one, the sinless one, took all our filth and all our grief and all our sins upon himself. "God made him, who had no sin, to become sin for us, so that in him we might become the righteousness of God" (2 Corinthians 5:21).

25. Galatians 2:21

26. Romans 5:6, 8, 10

27. Romans 5:1, 11

28. Romans 3:21–23

29. Romans 3:28

30. Romans 1:16–17. "It is by grace you have been saved, through faith—and this not from yourselves, it is the gift of God—not by works, so that no one can boast" (Ephesians 2:8). Salvation "does not depend on man's desire or effort, but on God's mercy" (Romans 9:16). When we were dead in our sins, "God made us alive with Christ. He forgave us all our sins, having cancelled the written code with its regulations, [that is, the law] that was against us and that stood opposed to us. He took it away, nailing it to the cross" (Colossians 2:13–14). We were dead in our sins—and could not make ourselves alive. "Like the rest, we were by nature objects of wrath. But because of his great LOVE for us, God, who is rich in mercy, made us alive with Christ,

even when we were dead in transgressions. It is by grace you have been saved" (Ephesians 2: 3–5)!

31. Romans 9:32; 10:3. Israel stumbled over the stumbling stone. Long ago God said, "See, I lay in Zion a stone that makes men stumble and a rock that makes them fall, but the one who trusts in him will never be put to shame" (Isaiah 8:14; 28:16). Who is that rock in whom men must trust? It is Jesus Christ.

32. Romans 7:12. "The law of the LORD is perfect, reviving the soul" (Psalm 19:7 NIV), or "converting the soul" (KJV).

33. Proverbs 11:21; Romans 6:23. "The way of the wicked will perish" (Psalm 1:6); but "blessed are they who walk according to the law of the LORD" (Psalm 119:2). "The LORD detests the way of the wicked, but he loves those who pursue righteousness" (Proverbs 15:9). "The truly righteous man attains life, but he who pursues evil goes to his death" (Proverbs 11:19). "Tell the righteous it will be well with them, for they will enjoy the fruit of their deeds. Woe to the wicked! Disaster is upon them! They will be paid back for what their hands have done" (Isaiah 3:10–11).

34. Romans 3:21, italics mine

35. See Romans 10:5–13

36. "The just shall live by faith (Habakkuk 2:4)!" These shining words were spoken by Habakkuk, an old covenant prophet, and his words were like golden keys to unlock the dark prison of death and damnation wherein God's holy law held us captive to await our just punishment.

37. Moses not only taught the doctrine of justification by faith, he also gave a great demonstration of it. The people had rebelled against God, so the LORD punished their sin by sending venomous snakes among them. God commanded the people who were bitten by the poisonous vipers to look at a bronze snake that Moses lifted up on a pole. The people must do this by faith, believing that this simple look would heal them and save them (see Numbers 21:4–9). This foreshadowed the raising of Christ on the cross. Jesus said: "Just as Moses lifted up the snake in the desert, so the Son of Man must be lifted up, that everyone who believes in him may have eternal life" (John 3:14).

38. Genesis 15:6

39. Romans 4:18, 20–24

40. There were serious charges against Moses; God said, "You did not trust in me. . . . You did not honour me as holy. . . . You broke faith with me in the presence of the Israelites. . . . You did not uphold my holiness among the Israelites" (Numbers 20:12; Deuteronomy 32:51).

41. Romans 4:6. "Blessed is the man whose transgressions are forgiven, whose sins are covered. Blessed is the man whose sin the LORD does not count against him" (Psalm 32:1–2).

42. Ezekiel 18:31, italics mine

43. Ezekiel 36:25–29, italics mine

44. One of the most amazing promises found in the old covenant Scriptures was God's promise to send his Holy Spirit to change us as part of the new covenant. God said, "In the last days I will pour out my spirit on all people. Your sons and daughters will prophesy; your young men will see visions; your old men will dream dreams. Even on my servants, both men and women, I will pour out my spirit in those days and they will prophesy" (Joel 2:28–32; see also Acts 2:17–21). God would pour out his Holy Spirit on the old and the young, on men and women, boys and girls, Jews and Gentiles. God's great and gracious work of regeneration—imparting new life, re-creating the human heart, and renewing the human mind—would know no boundaries!

45. 2 Corinthians 5:17–18

46. Ezekiel 36:26

47. Jesus is "the true light that gives light to every man" (John 1:9). Jesus himself said, "I am the light of the world. Whoever follows me will never walk in darkness, but will have the light of life. . . . I have come into the world as a light, so that no one who believes in me should stay in darkness" (John 8:12; 12:46). At one time, before we believed in Christ, "our foolish hearts were darkened"(Romans 1:21), but now God has "made his light shine in our hearts to give us the light of the knowledge of the glory of God in the face of Christ" (2 Corinthians 4:6). Our bodies do not glow with a heavenly light, but if Christ is in us, there is a divine light shining in our hearts. The new covenant Scriptures testify, "You were once darkness, but now you are light in the Lord" (Ephesians 5:8). Now that we are united to Christ and his Holy Spirit dwells in us, we become like him. Jesus said to his disciples, "You are the light of the world. . . . Let your light shine before men" (Matthew 5:14, 16).

48. Colossians 2:27

49. Romans 15:13; Colossians 2:7; Romans 5:5. The Word of God testifies, "You have been given fullness in Christ" (Colossians 2:9).

50. Psalm 14:1

51. Ephesians 2:12

52. Ephesians 2:2

53. 1 Corinthians 2:12

54. 1 Corinthians 2:16; 2 Corinthians 3:18

55. "We have this treasure in jars of clay to show that this all-surpassing power is from God and not from us. Though outwardly we are wasting away, yet inwardly we are being renewed day by day" (2 Corinthians 4:7, 16). These bodies of death (Romans 5:24), these "jars of clay" (2 Corinthians 4:7) that are so easily battered and shattered, these bodies created from the dust of the ground and so quickly returned to dust again (Genesis 2:7; 3:19; Psalm 90:3)—these bodies become God's dwelling place! "Don't

you know that you yourselves are God's temple and that God's Spirit lives in you? God's temple is sacred, and you are that temple. Do you not know that your body is a temple of the Holy Spirit, who is in you, whom you have received from God" (1 Corinthians 3:16; 6:19)?

56. Romans 8:4, 8–9. God also commands us to set our hearts and our minds on heavenly things, not on earthly things, "for you died, and your life is now hidden with Christ in God. Put to death, therefore, whatever belongs to your earthly nature . . . since you have taken off your old self with its practices and have put on the new self, which is being renewed in knowledge in the image of its creator. Let the peace of Christ rule in your hearts. . . . Let the word of Christ dwell in you richly" (see Colossians 3:3–16). Again God commands: "Put off your old self, which is being corrupted by its deceitful desires. . . . Be made new in the attitude of your minds. . . . Put on the new self, created to be like God in true righteousness and holiness" (Ephesians 4:22–24). "Do not conform any longer to the pattern of this world, but be transformed by the renewing of your mind" (Romans 12:2).

57. It is interesting to note the dictionary definition of the word "metamorphosis." It means "a change of form, shape or structure, with or without a change in nature." The transformation in the new covenant is different: There is no change in form; our bodies remain the same. But there is a change in nature, in the hidden realm of the heart, which can only be seen by the works that the changed heart produces.

Chapter 17: The Glorious Freedom of the Children of God

1. See Exodus 1:11–14
2. Exodus 2:23
3. Exodus 3:7, 10
4. Romans 8:21
5. John 1:12; Galatians 3:26. "How great is the LOVE that the Father has lavished on us, that we should be called children of God" (1 John 3:1)!
6. John 8:36
7. 1 John 3:5, 8; 1:7
8. John 8:34
9. "All have sinned and fallen short of the glory of God" (Romans 3:23). We are born into the slavery of sin. Each of us must confess: "Surely I was sinful at birth, sinful from the time my mother conceived me" (Psalm 51:5).
10. "Scripture declares that the whole world is a prisoner of sin" (Galatians 3:22).
11. Romans 6:12, 14; 7:14, 23. We also read that we were slaves to the one whom we obeyed—the tyrant called sin (Romans 6:16). We were controlled by the sinful nature (Romans 7:5). Sin bound us (Romans 7:6).
12. Ephesians 2:3, 12.
13. See Romans 5:6–10

14. See Romans 6:2–7. This is the great victory that overcomes the world—the faith in our hearts that Jesus is the Son of God, who died on the cross to save us from our sins. It is by God's grace that we have been saved, through this faith in Jesus. This faith is not from ourselves; it is the gift of God (Ephesians 2:8).

15. "I have been crucified with Christ and I no longer live, but Christ lives in me. The life I live in the body, I live by faith in the Son of God, who loved me and gave himself for me" (Galatians 2:20).

16. Romans 6:4–5. Paul continues, "If we died with Christ, we believe we will also live with him. . . . The death he died, he died to sin once for all; but the life he lives, he lives to God" (Romans 6:9–10).

17. 2 Corinthians 5:17

18. Galatians 5:1

19. Galatians 5:24. "Those who belong to Christ Jesus have crucified the sinful nature with its passions and desires" (Galatians 5:13).

20. Revelation 1:5–6

21. Deuteronomy 6:5

22. Matthew 3:15

23. Matthew 5:17–18

24. Romans 7:6; Galatians 5:18; Romans 6:14

25. Colossians 2:17

26. In this sense too, Christ fulfilled the law, by paying the penalty for sin.

27. Romans 7:4–6. "If you are led by the Spirit, *you are not under law*" (Galatians 5:18, italics mine)! Now we seek to be justified not by keeping the law, but by believing in Christ. "I *died to the law*, so that I might live for God. . . . I do not set aside the grace of God, for if righteousness could be gained through the law, Christ died for nothing" (Galatians 2:19–21, italics mine).

28. Galatians 4:3; 3:23

29. Romans 8:21. Remember what Jesus himself said: "If the Son shall set you free, you shall be free indeed" (John 8:36)!

30. See Galatians 5:1–5

31. Christ Jesus has become "our righteousness, holiness, and redemption" (1 Corinthians 1:30). In him we are made "the righteousness of God" (2 Corinthians 5:21).

32. Luke 1:75

33. See Colossians 1:19–23

34. "He forgave us all our sins, having cancelled the written code with its regulations [that is, the law] that was against us and that stood opposed to us; he took it away, nailing it to the cross" (Colossians 2:13–14). In Christ we have a great advocate, our great High Priest, who intercedes for us continually before the throne of God; but

human beings also have a great adversary, "that ancient serpent called the devil or Satan," who accuses us day and night before God (Revelation 12:9–10). The name Satan actually means "The Accuser" and he legitimately had charges against us, because we all had broken God's law. We all were sinful—sinful from birth, sinful by nature, sinful in our thoughts, words and deeds. Satan had legitimate claim upon our souls, but Christ conquered the devil and his demons, "triumphing over them by the cross" (Colossians 2:15). "Who then will bring any charge against those whom God has chosen? It is God who justifies! Who is the one that condemns? Christ Jesus, who died—more than that, who was raised to life— is at the right hand of God and is also interceding for us! Who shall separate us from the LOVE of Christ?" The devil? Never! "For I am convinced that neither death nor life, neither angels nor demons [nor the devil himself] neither the present nor the future, nor any powers [no, not all the demonic powers of hell] neither height nor depth, nor anything else in all creation, will be able to separate us from the LOVE of God that is in Christ Jesus our Lord" (Romans 8:33–39). It is our union with Christ—the fact that we are "in Christ" by faith—that saves us and frees us from condemnation.

35. Romans 10:4; 8:1

36. Psalm 89:48

37. Romans 8:3; Hebrews 2:9

38. Romans 1:4. Jesus himself said that this would be the great sign proving that he was who he claimed to be. He said, "Destroy this temple and I will raise it again in three days." The temple of which he spoke was his body—he was referring to his resurrection from the dead. (See John 2:18–22).

39. Isaiah 25:7–8. The Psalmist also testifies, "Our God is a God who saves; from the Sovereign LORD comes escape from death" (Psalm 68:20).

40. Isaiah 9:2, 6. He would be the Son of God, "being in very nature God"— but he would be "made in human likeness . . . being found in appearance as a man" (Philippians 2:7).

41. Hebrews 2:14–15

42. 1 Corinthians 15:26; Romans 6:9

43. 1 Corinthians 15:54–57

44. John 5:21, 24–26

45. John 11:25–26. To prove the truth of his word and the power of his promise, Jesus then called forth a man from his tomb—a man whose body had already begun to decay. Jesus raised him from the dead and freed him from his grave. See John 11:38–44.

46. Romans 7:20. God's Word declares this truth: "The wages of sin is death" (Romans 6:23). Even when we desire to do good, even when we delight in God's law, "evil is right there with me . . . in the members of my body" (Romans 7:21–22). At

times, there seems to be a war raging within us, a war between good and evil, so that we cry out in despair: "Who will rescue me from this body of death?" Thanks be to God! There is an answer, a Saviour, and victory through Jesus Christ our Lord! Although sin remains in us, in our bodies, "there is now no condemnation for those who are in Christ Jesus" (Romans 8:1). And his holy Spirit now resides in us, so that "through Christ Jesus the law of the Spirit of life set me free from the law of sin and death" (Romans 8:2).

47. Romans 8:10–11. Yes, sin remains in our bodies, but we now live according to God's Spirit within us. "Those who live according to the sinful nature have their minds set on what that nature desires; but those who live in accordance with the Spirit have their minds set on what the Spirit desires. The mind of sinful man is death, but the mind controlled by the Spirit is life and peace. The sinful mind is hostile to God. It does not submit to God's law, nor can it do so. Those controlled by the sinful nature cannot please God. You [who believe in Jesus], however, are controlled not by the sinful nature, but by the Spirit, if the Spirit of God lives in you" (Romans 8:5–9).

48. Romans 8:21

49. "For in this hope we were saved. But hope that is seen is no hope at all. Who hopes for what he already has? But if we hope for what we do not have, we wait for it patiently" (Romans 8:24–25).

50. Revelation 1:18

51. Revelation 21:3–4

52. Revelation 22:20–21

53. Psalm 118:5–6